THE POLISHING CLOTH

EDITORS: REGINALD ABBOTT, RUPERT DUPREE, SHANE BRUCE

GEORGIA STATE UNIVERSITY'S PERIMETER COLLEGE

Kendall Hunt
publishing company

Kendall Hunt
publishing company

www.kendallhunt.com
Send all inquiries to:
4050 Westmark Drive
Dubuque, IA 52004-1840

ISBN: 978-1-5249-8007-8

Published in the United States of America

Contents

Editor's Note

This is the Twenty-Fourth Edition of *The Polishing Cloth.*

This is the **Editorial Board** for the Twenty-Fourth Edition of *The Polishing Cloth.*

And now, on with the show. . .

Reginald Abbott, PhD
Rooster Village Farm
October 2018

Part One

SHINY

Haiti: A Life-Changing Trip

by Mylena Moretti

"Do not waste time bothering whether you 'love' your neighbor; act as if you did."
from *Mere Christianity* (1952) by C. S. Lewis

Social justice is something I would definitely say has been part of my upbringing since it can be defined as how a human being decides the way one lives life by either bringing equality to society or benefit from resources. As a child, I saw both poverty and wealth, which made me question why things were that way. I did not understand how some individuals could have so much, and how some did not even have the basic resources needed to survive. In July 2013, I snapped out of my questioning but complacent mindset and decided to volunteer in Porto Principe, Haiti. As a result, my perspective of the world changed. While in Haiti, I spent an entire day at an orphanage with some amazing children. This experience would change my life forever.

Haiti is a beautiful island where people go to enjoy a stunning blue sea. Although it has its beauty, life is very hard for some natives who live there. Basic resources needed to survive, such as enough meals, hygiene products, and water, are not available for everybody. On the seventh day of my trip, a group of volunteers and I went to an orphanage called Canaa. It is located in the middle of nowhere. It looks like a desert because it is surrounded by sand. There is a huge tent that houses a lot of people underneath. The heat that day was overbearing, and it made many of us dehydrated.

The team and I went to the orphanage to entertain and to play with the children. There were a couple of teenagers playing drums and a guitar, which was very odd for a place that lacked basic resources. They were playing Christian songs, and it was awesome to see that these teenagers were able to learn how to play these instruments. It was even better that they used their new skill to entertain us. At some point, we started to sing and dance with the children. It had become even hotter with such a large number of people in the tent. I would say that there were over a hundred people mixed between middle-aged women and children. The majority were children who looked happy because they were smiling and wanted to be hugged whenever they could. In a place where there was not enough food to eat, no comfortable or decent seats to accommodate everybody, and where the word "air conditioner" was far away from having even a room in one's mind, there were tears of joy and big smiles on the faces of individuals expressing their gratitude. It was delightful to learn that I could live with less in order to help someone who does not have a lot.

Later, I saw a man standing in front of the tent with the teenagers. This old gentleman was wearing a long-sleeved dress shirt and glasses. Someone told me that he was the director of the orphanage and had a restaurant downtown. I hesitated a little, but I finally mustered up the courage to go and speak to him. I was eager to find out his motivation for starting the orphanage. He was so kind when I approached.

"Hello, Sir. It's nice to meet you," I said.

"Hi, Miss, it's nice to meet you too. How are you doing today?"

We started to talk. As the conversation went on, I could see his eyes lighting up about the whole moment. I asked:

"Sir, if you don't mind, what motivated you to open an orphanage?"

"Well, for me, it's about the difference that I can make in someone else's life. I have a business downtown. And part of my small profit I used to buy those instruments, so I would be able to teach these guys how to play. And their future could possibly be different from the majority; consequently, they will make a difference later on in life."

My overall experience at Canaa and my talk with its director taught me of social justice. I realized that my environment can be a better place in which to live based on my decisions, such as not buying more than I need. Equally important, I learned how I can be the change that I expect instead of living and just dreaming about a great world to be in. When one individual decides to go against the average system and change the way he lives, a group of people who are in need can be helped, and the world could possibly change for the better. Some have a lot, but are still ungrateful. On the other hand, some have nothing, but are able to live amazing moments like the children at the Canaa Orphanage who were singing and dancing to the music. Our very small act of kindness or generosity begins a cycle that may not have an end. As C. S. Lewis says, we should not ask about love; instead, we should live love.

Different From My Mother

by Virginia Edwards

I am often startled by how dissimilar I am to my mother. We argue and it usually results in my struggling to understand why her expectations of me are different than my own. Of course, we love each other, but it can be difficult to understand one another when we come from different backgrounds and were reared differently. My mother was born in the early 1960s, so she is part of the Baby Boomer Generation. I, on the other, was born in 1995 at Grady Memorial Hospital where I officially became a part of the Millennial Generation. My mother's generation lived in a time when people had different ideals, traditions, and values compared to my generation today. Understanding these differences between our upbringings has helped me to understand the differences that I see between me and my mother.

My mother was always proactive, never waiting for anything. After graduation, she was offered a scholarship to Emory University, and she immediately switched schools, homes, and states to attend. My mother worked to support herself through college, took a full class load every semester, and never got below a B, except for one C in Biology. She started her own landscaping company and determined that she was ready to be married. I, however, am a procrastinator. No doubt, my generation has had this effect on me: slow down, resist aging, and, most importantly, resist responsibility. After high school, I was at a loss, for I had no sense of direction, no passions, and no motivation to put in the hard work that it would take to attend another grueling few years of school.

So, I took time off. This seemed to upset my mother who thought it best to attend classes while I figured out what I wanted to do with the rest of my life. After taking time off, I did eventually attend a local college, only to stop after a mere two semesters. Yet again, I would take time off from school, this time for two years before the drive kicked up in me to go back. I am almost twenty-three now. I am still years away from obtaining my dream degree; I have no plans to marry or hopes of being married in the next few years; I do not own my own company, know how to run one, or even want one. Consequently, I do not feel anywhere close to the level of maturity that my mother displayed at my age. These major differences in our lives have made it challenging for both of us to relate to one another's situations.

Today, children grow up in homes supported by credit cards and borrowed money. It was important when my parents met that their finances be in order before they married in order to avoid debt and to provide for their growing family. I am constantly being nagged about my finances at this point in my life. My generation does not think in terms of preparing for sixty years from now, which is ironic because our life expectancy rate is continuously rising. Our parents and grandparents experienced the Great Depression and the years of havoc it created afterwards. There seems to be a growing gap between the number of people concerned with having a savings account and retirement plan and those having nothing to rely on at all.

The Millennial Generation lacks responsibility for its people and expects government programs to bail them out. I am well aware of the fact that our generation will continue to experience the trend of not making as much as our parents' generation did, and, yes, it does scare me. Does it scare me enough to start saving right away? Sadly, it does not. I still live the reckless paycheck-to-paycheck lifestyle. I am certainly not like my frugal mother, for I am a swiping machine swiping every last penny away. As my mother likes to say, "It is called growing up without."—something that I, she adds, "know nothing about."

Still, my mother's traditions, values, and opinions matter more to me than anyone else's. Our arguments are nothing more than manifestations of misunderstandings about one another. My desire is to bridge the gaps between me and my mother. However, we cannot understand each other entirely without having experienced what the other has. We can only try to sympathize and find common scenarios that relate to each other's current or past situation. No matter what our differences are, I will always love and respect my mother; it is because of her that I am who I am today.

Melting the Ice Away

by Andrew Ford

Topic: "In the midst of winter, I finally learned that there was in me an invincible summer."
—Albert Camus Discuss.

When thinking of winter, one's mind conjures up images of cold, dark isolation. It is the season when living beings are suddenly surrounded by frigid darkness and every day is a struggle to survive. In the same way that our Earth experiences winter, so does our condition in this life. A winter in one's life is to be expected, accepted, and endured, the same as in the winter season of any given year. However, it sometimes becomes difficult to realize one's ability to survive this state of mind.

Winter in our life comes from both the events that affect our lives every day and how we cope with these events. In some cases (such as my own), an incorrect balance of chemicals may make winter seem inescapable. My winter started in elementary school and did not end until my sophomore year of high school. As a child, I was quite energetic and outgoing. This, coupled with my serious need for speech therapy, made me an easy target for harassment. Because of the discouragement that I felt while speaking at all, my outgoing, bubbly personality fizzled into nihilism and isolation. My speech improved, but what I thought were witty remarks turned quickly into angry cynicism. I would barricade myself in my bedroom most days feeling hopeless that I could ever get better. So, I finally sought some outside help.

After my first visit to the psychiatrist, I was diagnosed with depression and anxiety. I was then immediately prescribed a daily forty-milligram dose of Prozac. I was told that I may feel "strange" for the first two weeks and that this was "normal." Instead of feeling "strange" or "normal," I had no emotion at all. I felt hollow, with no motivation to try at school, to make friends, or to play music as I had so loved to do. When I expressed my concerns to my psychiatrist, she seemed to have an immediate solution. It was Xanax. My SSRI dependency was quickly replaced by a benzo dependency that bottomed me out even worse than the Prozac. I realized at that point that I could no longer look for help from the outside. I had to help myself.

After a long transition, I was finally able to stop taking medication and pursue my passions. I immersed myself in my music and humor; moreover, I, through them, was able to communicate better than ever before. This led to my meeting other artists and musicians with similar experiences and forming incredibly strong friendships. With every show that I played, I could feel winter's snow melting away to reveal a summer that shone bright enough to dissolve my icy perceptions about myself.

The potential to change the seasons of my life was within me the whole time. I allowed my passion to burn as hot as the sun and that is what began the summer of my life that I enjoy today. I am not naïve to the fact that winter may start to creep in again at some point. Perhaps it will come in the near future. The difference is that I now know that my ability to melt the ice away will never leave me.

The Light of Happiness

by Leu Nubete

It was the summer of 2012, and I was finally able to visit my home country of Ethiopia. I had not been there since I was eight, so I decided to go back and visit my old house. When I finally stood face-to-face with my past life, I could not believe that I was finally back. The hot air whooshed by while I looked at the curvy, worn-down outlines of my former dwelling. An orange light illuminated the scene. As the rusty house gates opened slowly across the gravel, the light grew brighter and warmer. A new face greeted me with a smile. Eden, the tenant, had been living there while we were away. As I walked through the door, I immediately spotted the banana trees mother and I had planted next to the gates before we left. I went up and felt the large, leafy stems that had grown four times their size since I last saw them. Beside them were the pomegranate trees that smelled as sweet as fresh honey. As a child, I used to shake the trees until a pomegranate fell from the top and cracked open upon the ground. I enjoyed the addictive taste of the sweet and sour fruit until I had a sugar rush. The lovely winds carried the smells of the fruit around the house for everyone to catch a whiff. My favorite place in the whole house is at the center of the trees that surround it. At that moment, just as it had in the past, my fireplace brought a sense of happiness and tranquility to my soul as if it were a place of meditation. From the moment I saw it, I immediately felt a calm satisfaction. I was where I loved to be. The fire is my favorite place because it was where I ate great food, petted animals, and met with friends and family.

I walked into my room to put down my luggage. The walls, colored crimson red, looked as fresh as when I had last seen them. Red was and still is my favorite color. It reminded me of the flames that shed their light on my house every night. As I stared at my rugged bed, my nose caught a scent of my favorite food that I had not consumed in years. My stomach growled like a wild hyena that had not found a meal in days. Our cook, Selam, had just finished making spaghetti from the fresh, red tomatoes that had grown in our garden behind the pomegranate trees. I could already taste the sauce before I even took a bite. The house had been stuffed with the aroma, and the thought of eating made my stomach growl even more. As she used to when I was a young boy, Selam knocked on our room doors and told my siblings and me to come around the hearth to grab a bite. I opened the red doors and walked straight down the brick stairs towards the fire. The hot blaze was a nice touch to the cold night. An assemblage of logs was surrounded by a circular stone foundation. It resembled the top part of a water well. We grabbed a couple of wooden stools my father had made before we had left for America, and we ate together, feasting on the spaghetti our mouths had not met in years. My mother let out a "Wow!" She added, "I've never been so happy from tasting food before." Selam replied back with a devilish grin and a kind nod. After I had washed my plate that I had already cleaned with my fork, I decided to take a short nap to let the food settle down.

When I woke up, I ran back down the brick stairs to see if anyone was still there. No one was. The sun had fully set, and the fire was roaring. I sat on the wooden stool I had left before I went to sleep. I looked into the flames and thought about the memories I had of this one area. When I was a child, I used to have my most noteworthy conversations and laughs with friends and family here. I remember the day when I asked my cook to show me a magic trick. She took burning coal that glowed as red as lava from the crackling fire and put it in her mouth. I was eager to try it myself, but she would not let me. The fireplace, this time, was lit with yellow flames and felt almost as if it were comforting me by wrapping a warm blanket of smoke around my body. My sister and mother came back down because they could not sleep, and Selam came back with juice. She had made it for the next day, but since almost everyone was up, she poured us all a cup. After a while, our stomachs started to growl. We ate around the fire so much that our minds would feel hunger whenever we sat around it.

My mother decided to make some steak. She set a large frying pan on the crackling blaze. The steak sizzled as she flipped and tossed the beef around the pan, and my sister grabbed a few wooden stools for herself, my mother, and Selam. We talked about our day, drank freshly squeezed juice, and ate the succulent steak. The dark, mysterious clouds were covering the moon that night, and the fire was our only source of light. We invited our old friends to the house to sit with them to talk like we used to and share all the food we had made. I had not seen them in years, so it felt like a family reunion. We told jokes we used to tell, along with many conversations about everything: the time we stole back my action figure from our neighbors, all the things we had missed while we were gone, and our goals for the future. We resembled a rowdy bunch of cavemen who were chuckling and cooking hunted meat, amused by the fire we had just discovered. After the reunion was over, I went back to my room for bed. I could not wait to see what tomorrow night had in store.

The next day, as I watched the sunset while sitting on the brick stairs, the winds started to cool. A cold chill whooshed its way around my cheeks and made my teeth chatter. I heard the sound of clucking echoing through the thin walls of my room. The chickens were still up. They lived in a surrounding of small wooden fences at the right end next to my room. Their long, soft, white feathers stood out from the dirt and gravel. It was unreal to see a live chicken because I hadn't come across one since I had left Ethiopia. I picked one up and took it to the fire to have some company. While I was gently rubbing its feathers, it oddly turned its neck and closed its eyes. I could tell it felt comfortable because it had stopped clucking and flapping its angel-like wings. I recollected the memories of all the animals I used to pet sitting next to the fire. These animals included two dogs, two turtles, one goat, one monkey, and my fat cat.

My furry cat, now dead, was my favorite pet. I thought about the days when my cat would chase me around the house when I was eight. I would run for my life, screaming and sweating, until her tiny feet could not keep up her large belly any longer. It was our daily exercise. It would almost never let me pet its furry, white body because it was indeed an evil feline. But whenever we sat next to the fire, even the cat could not resist being happy. I would sometimes feed it fish that I had taken from the hob, and it would purr from the delight of fresh food. Then, and only then, would it let me pet its smooth fur without any complaints. Its fat would jiggle whenever I patted its body, and my friends and family would laugh whenever I displayed it to them. I would also chug a bottle of Coca-Cola and shake my belly so they could hear the liquid splashing around my stomach. We were the entertainment. Thinking about these kind times made my eyes as red as a tomato, and my ears feel warm as if they had just bathed in the sun. This was why around the fire was my favorite place to stay.

Revisiting my fireplace is a goal I would like to accomplish in the next few years. Not only was it a place with excellent fruits and odd pets, but it was also a place where I could unwind and have fun with friends and family. A place like that cannot be replicated quickly, and it is one of the most important parts of my life. I will never forget those rusty gates, the tall trees that I used to walk past every day, and the fireplace I sat next to every night. It was a site where I could enjoy food, have fun with friends and family, or make party dances with my pets. No matter who you are or where you live, there will always be a special place that is dear to you. Mine is unique and unreplaceable. I will cherish this home for the rest of my days.

Coca-Cola's Subliminal Efforts to Unify the World

by Rachael Derby

It is one of the most popular beverages in the world that seems to show up on time to every party, every family get-together, every loud sports event, and every popcorn and movie night around the globe. Something as small as a bottle of Coke has traveled globally for many years in an effort to unite people of different cultures and ethnicities in this divided world. Coca-Cola's vision is to highlight the principle that even though the world is filled with diversity and differences, we are all humans trying to live through the hard times to get to the enjoyable ones.

Curiosity led me and my cousins from Texas to the World of Coca-Cola Museum in Atlanta. I had never been although I have lived in the greater Atlanta area for a while now, and my cousins had never been either. When we walked up to the entrance, we noted that the entire building and all the things around it were painted red and white. I began to realize that Coca-Cola was not simply a carbonated beverage in America but a worldwide company as well. We headed toward the friendly associate at the ticket booth and gave him our tickets for admittance. While we waited somewhat patiently in line to get into the main exhibit, the fizz-pop sounds of the opening of a fresh can of Coca-Cola played nonstop on a speaker overhead. The snapping sounds of lifted pop tabs and the crackling noise of the tiny carbonated bubbles as they leap out of the can and to the surface made me wish for an ice-cold Coca-Cola.

We only waited for about a few minutes, while my cousin endlessly fixed her lip gloss, before we were greeted by unusually friendly associates and managers inside the building. They handed us miniature cans of Coca-Cola and even offered to open them for us too. Once inside, I took in all the details of the lobby and its plush red carpet under my new shoes. To my left, there were many different-sized, HD television screens, and one screen was an unusually skinny, vertical rectangle. No matter the size or shape, every television played the Coca-Cola commercial and proclaimed the slogan "Taste the Feeling." in different languages from around the world. I took an unconscious sip of the Coke in my hand. The commercial showed the Coke being ceremoniously poured into a tall glass of ice cubes. By the end of the clip, the glass was so full that the carbonated beverage began to spill over the edge of the glass containing it. At that moment, I, my relatives, and the other tourists were very glad to have that mini-can of Coke in hand as we were all being hypnotized by the dark amber liquid. On the far wall to my right, there was a large timer that was slowly counting down the minutes until the next self-guided tour. The excitement was starting to build, and the chatter of both tourists and locals started to get louder. The long minutes decreased to seconds and then finally to zeros. Then, the wait was over and everyone was allowed into the next part of the exhibit.

We walked downhill through the automatic doors, taking quick pictures for our high-priority Snapchat stories, and were then led to a smaller transition room that was filled with memorabilia. Yellowed paper advertisements in one showcase depicted young people smiling while happily sharing a Coke in a staged and synchronized fashion. In addition, everything was so closely packed together that the wall beneath was barely visible. Our tour guide introduced herself and gave a brief speech about the different tales behind each of the historic Coca-Cola products and flyers. She even pointed out the former Coca-Cola sign that used to stand proudly on the beverage's corporate building. As I looked closely at the sign, I could see hail dents on it, each having stolen a proud bit of Coca-Cola history. Once everybody had a chance to look around, we were ushered into a large, dimly-lit movie theatre where our guide presented a short film.

I slid along the glossy floor between the rows of seats and sat down in a cushiony chair between my cousin Kevin and my identical twin

Amanda. The theatre became a hall of shadows as the lights slowly faded away. Darkness along with her twin Silence filled the massive room. I found myself sinking down into my seat in response as I longed for comforting things, such as soft blankets made of cotton. As images scrolled aimlessly through my head, I found the film superficially jovial and, to a degree, subliminally eerie. The word "eerie" crossed my mind because the film presented everyone with a can of Coke as suddenly joyful. In the film, all of the people who had a Coke in hand were frowning or unhappy for split seconds, and then all unhappiness vanished instantly once the Coca-Cola came. I blinked twice to clear my eyes of the over-exaggeration that seemed to stick to my eyelids.

The movie portrayed the people who had a Coca-Cola as "happy go lucky" people who indeed were having a great time all the time. However, one thing was very evident throughout the film, and that was the diversity of the people in it. The film showed many sorts of people and cultures from around the world celebrating life's best moments, each in their own special Coke-added way. I sat up abruptly. I could sense the pupils of my green eyes closing to mere specks as I tried to capture all of the bright images that had caught my attention. Movies nowadays do not have this much diversity, so I believe that is why it gripped my attention so quickly. The film also universally linked Coca-Cola with simple but significant cheerful times (e.g. engagements, marriage, high school proms, Christmas, etc.) that the audience could relate to and become sentimental over while they considered their own lives. After the film was over, it left me reminiscing about some of the meaningful and memorable things in my own life.

After the film, we walked into a larger room where someone dressed in a plush polar bear costume with an especially artificial smile plastered on it waved at us. I felt a strange sense of welcome from that bear. The room was very large and the ceiling soared into the sky as massive windows let in the sunlight at every angle. In front of me, I could see a large decal on the wall that read, "Whether crushed or intact, whether seen in light or felt in darkness, the Coca-Cola bottle can be recognized worldwide." Of course, since I am a young adult, I do not remember the original glass Coca-Cola bottle being the norm. We later sauntered into the section of the exhibit where the history of Coca-Cola was presented behind tall, Plexiglas cabinets. There was a fancy counter made of marble to my left which was a recreation of a soda fountain of decades ago. My cousins, my sister, and I took both candid and posed (again, high-priority) Instagram-worthy pictures and then we moved on. As I wandered through this maze-like portion of the exhibit, I saw relics older than I am, and I learned how factory workers in the past made Coca-Cola by hand.

When I strolled past one exhibit, I caught sight of my reflection in a cloudy mirror atop a nineteenth-century vanity. I stopped to stare at the fading spine-chilling portraits that hung on each wall. The faces in these pictures seemed as though they wanted to bore holes into my soul. These people were part of some hierarchy that had nothing to do with me. As I stepped nearer, I looked at my reflection in this historical recreation, and I realized that my ancestors from the Caribbean would never have been able to look in this same mirror. To the left of the mirror lay a vintage, bristled hairbrush that matched the small floral-patterned vanity table. The star of the show, an empty, old Coca-Cola bottle with a torn label, sat proudly in the center of the small table. I suddenly came to the realization like a slap in the face that Coca-Cola was not always universally available for everyone, yet it had seemed that way all along in the film. My heart picked up speed. The fact that this inequality had been unacknowledged in the film was striking. Coca-Cola has not had a blameless history, yet any inequalities were brushed aside for the "happiness" that had taken their place. Certain portions of history were pushed aside, swept up, and discarded. I began to understand why: Those times were very disheartening. However, without that unmentioned history, we would not be where we are today. Coca-Cola did not start off spreading happiness, and it saddened me to come to this stark conclusion. I continued to puzzle over the encased room with floral wallpaper, and I wished I could reach out and touch some of the prized objects. As I stared into the center of a single flower on the wall paper, I seriously wondered why skin color or culture could cause division and prejudice. I was mere inches away from the glass, yet I was still so far from any further discoveries. My twin sister called out to me and I peeled my now clammy hands from the clear glass leaving my thoughts and realizations at the vanity table.

After the eye-opening historical portion of my self-guided tour, my sister, my cousins and I headed over to the tasting section of the World of

Coca-Cola. A long conveyor belt carrying Coca-Cola bottles hummed as it moved steadily overhead in the spacious room. I pondered how happiness could come in bottles as my brand-new shoes stuck with every step to the unbelievably sticky floor. Caffeinated, hyperactive children ran about the room non-stop, and I smiled while politely dodging the crazy fun as parents scooped each child up. I looked about the large room with its different and unique Coca-Cola company beverages from the globe, and was amazed at how Coca-Cola products had managed to make it onto every continent in an effort to undo the world's differences. Then, my sister pointed out one soda in particular called "Beverly" that I had to try. Hesitantly, I grabbed a cup and poured some "Beverly" out of the dispenser into my cup. I took a small sip, and the pungent taste of the soda set fire to my throat as it went down. It was as if I had swallowed some strong mouthwash. My jokester of a sister snickered at my sour expression and we headed over to another station to try some more sodas from Asia. I resolved never again to drink "Beverly."

After we left the World of Coca-Cola, a few things stuck with me. For example, just like a smile, Coca-Cola is recognized around the world. It was not always like that before, but the progress made by this company since its beginnings is remarkable. From what I have gathered, it appears that the company does not want the world to fall back into those dark and divided times again either. Furthermore, that is the reason they place their focus away from a more accurate background and onto diversity and happiness instead. Something as miniscule as a bottle of Coke has traveled around the world in an effort both to unite people of different cultures and ethnicities and to promote the idea that, even if we live in other countries or have different cultural/ethnic backgrounds, we are all humans just trying to live life. We all want to get through the difficulties to celebrate the successes. And I believe that this is what they mean when they softly intone their slogan "Taste the Feeling."

Work Cited

"The World of Coca-Cola." The World of Coca-Cola, Atlanta, 19 Sept. 2017. Exhibition.

How Creativity Can Enhance Sustainability A Review of Daan Roosegaarde's "A Smog Vacuum Cleaner and Other Magical City Designs"

by Ayesha Siddiqa

Can we all live in a world where sustainability and creativity are our true capital? According to Dutch artist Daan Roosegaarde in "A Smog Vacuum Cleaner and Other Magical City Designs," we most definitely can. Roosegaarde argues that by continually asking ourselves questions and using creative thinking to find the solutions, in time and with the help of people, we can slowly restore our planet. By successfully developing projects that are merged with technology and art, his works connect people and creativity to improve the daily lives of citizens residing in urban environments all around the world. He mentions that something as simple as a way of thinking triggers a response from us. Roosegaarde also informs his audience that he and his team know ways to transform polluted urban areas so that we can become aware of our surroundings. He consistently states his arguments using several persuasive methods that solidify his ideas about reducing pollution on a large scale by utilizing images, reliability, and emotionally-charged words.

Roosegaarde displays various images as he talks about his creations and ideas regarding making our future energy friendly. He first speaks about his project with the Van Gogh Foundation to bring the renowned artist's presence back to the Netherlands. Roosegaarde grasps the audience's attention by talking about glow-in-the-dark stars, something that was a part of almost everyone's childhood. He explains how he was inspired by something so simple and created a bicycle path on local grounds that charged via sunlight and glowed at night, thereby recreating Van Gogh's *Starry Night* (1889). The reason he starts off with this specific accomplishment is to draw the audience in and trigger their interest with the spectacular images of the illuminated paths. Roosegaarde then smoothly transitions into his central topic, smog control. He shows the audience two images he took in Beijing, China. One picture was taken on a weekend, where the sky looked clear, while the second picture showed dense layers of smog which was normal for any weekday in Beijing.

The drastic difference between these two visuals provoked an emotional response of uneasiness from the audience since the displayed images showed them the disastrous damage pollution was capable of. After seeing Beijing's smog and its potential to harm future generations, Roosegaarde was inspired to create a smog vacuum cleaner that collected polluted air and released it as clean air. He then shows a small amount of the particles the vacuum collected: "This is Beijing's smog. This is in our lungs right now. If you live next to a highway, it's the same as seventeen cigarettes per day." Again, a sense of alarm spread amongst the audience when they were shown the particles, but, regardless, they stay engaged with the speaker because they were entirely captivated by his way of thinking. As a group, the images aided Roosegaarde in his initial argument about building towards a clean and eco-friendly future.

The talk remained lighthearted as Roosegaarde kept his speech conversational rather than formal and continuously interacted with his audience. By doing this, he portrays himself as someone who is open-minded and easy-going. This increases the chance of the audience being persuaded and remaining engrossed as he talks. When speaking about what occurs when an individual presents a new idea, Roosegaarde posed a question to the audience, "There's this weird tendency to reply to every new idea starting with two words. Which are?" Several people in the crowd took part in responding to the question. This not only makes the speaker more appealing, but it also makes him seem reliable and genuine. As his position as a speaker, Roosegaarde does not force any of his argument or way of thinking onto anyone. Instead, he takes his time in explaining his thoughts while including the spectators as well. Eventually, a bond begins to form, and the speaker's arguments become more persuasive.

Roosegaarde used emotionally charged words to further explain the need to live sustainably. He accomplished this by referring to his creation *Waterlicht* (2015), which is a combination of LEDs and lenses demonstrating how high the water levels would rise if people all around the world stopped their efforts towards leading sustainable lives. Roosegaarde stated that "if, today, we all go home, and we say, 'Oh, whatever, somebody else will do it for us.' or 'We'll wait for government or whomever.' You know, we're not going to do that. It goes wrong." He uses these charged words to initiate an understanding and build up the idea that we should try our absolute best to support and promote sustainable lifestyles and not wait on others to take action to fix our mistakes. He persuades the audience in a way that they feel included in an ongoing movement that can eventually launch us into a future of endless possibilities.

The initial persuasive message in Roosegaarde's talk was that even the smallest idea, if adequately implemented, could generate change. By building up his ideas with his spectators, Roosegaarde delivered his argument effectively. He proved it to be logical and systematic by encouraging people to be curious and take action on their curiosity. His explanation immensely persuaded the audience that we are not merely consumers; instead, we are the creators. By merging creativity and sustainability on a global scale, we can move forward as we influence and envision a bright future.

Work Cited

Roosegaarde, Daan. "A Smog Vacuum Cleaner and Other Magical City Designs." *TED2017*, 26 April 2017, Vancouver, British Columbia, www.ted.com. Accessed 23 Apr. 2018. Conference Presentation.

"The Future of Plastic Recycling" A Review of Mike Biddle's "We Can Recycle Plastic"

by Ayston Scully

In the 1970s, the concerns of people all over the world, but especially in the United States, about the effects of human consumption and corporate emissions arose as part of a movement to address the impact of human activity on the earth. It was during this revolution that recycling, now a common practice in cities and countries around the world, began. Despite decades of investment and lobbying, there are still many holes in the process of recycling, especially plastic recycling. In "We Can Recycle Plastic" (*TEDGlobal 2011 Conference*, Edinburgh, Scotland), Mike Biddle addresses the issues of plastic recycling and explains the health and environmental issues which are a result of the current system for disposing of plastic waste in the West. Biddle uses both emotional and logical reasoning to argue that it is the moral obligation of the consumer both to understand where trash goes and to buy products that are sustainably made. Although he neglects to identify the financial difficulties of selling recycled plastics for reuse, he successfully convinces the audience that repurposed plastic products are the only way to sustain a consumer society.

In "We Can Recycle Plastic," Biddle uses quantifiable data to appeal to his audience in a logical manner, which legitimizes the argument that the effects of mass consumerism have detrimental effects on the environment and people living in developing countries. Biddle states that, according to the United Nations, "eighty-five billion pounds of electronic waste gets discarded each and every year." These numbers are staggering, but more importantly they support Biddle's argument by citing factual evidence. In addition, by referencing United Nations data, he strengthens the credibility of his claim and blocks counter arguments that the rate at which consumers, especially consumers in the West, dispose of goods is insignificant.

Biddle then uses photos and stories to appeal to the audience on an emotional level. Through evoking despair and disgust in his audience, he motivates outrage at consumer behaviors which destroy environmental landscapes and exploit people living in poverty-stricken places. The photos that Biddle chooses show mountains of trash that have taken over thousands of acres of the earth. In so doing, he shows his audience the horrifying consequences of the extensive use of plastics.

Biddle combines an optimistic tone with evidence of current technology to prove to the audience that repurposing plastic waste is a feasible method to produce new products. He introduces the audience to "the future of plastic recycling" by enthusiastically describing how these technologies can end the devastation that plastic waste has on the world and its people. Biddle explains that he has already created a recycling plant which turns the plastic found in "above-ground mines" into pellets that can be used to create new products. The description of this new process not only suggests that people can now buy sustainable products but also that this is a growing industry which could soon be the sole way that plastic products are produced in the near future. If the use of plastic waste to create new products had not already been developed and were not already in limited use, then people would find it harder to see the effects that this process, if made mandatory, could have in a short period of time.

Although informative, Biddle's talk also seems to be a marketing tactic. He uses his remarks to interest companies in his recycled plastic as source material and introduces individuals to the possibility of buying products manufactured using plastics created by his technology. He fails to address the issue that using recycled material might not be the most cost-effective way for companies to make their products. Companies are constantly buying the cheapest raw materials in order to widen their profit margin. The cost of processing recycled products is high, which makes the plastic pellets made out of repurposed plastic hard to compete with "virgin" pellets.

Biddle's "We Can Recycle Plastics" uses logical and emotional modes of persuasion to support the argument that it is the moral obligation of the users of plastic products to be knowledgeable about plastic production and behave in ways that reduce the environmental and social effects which are a consequence of large-scale plastic consumption. He touches on all aspects of the human psyche to support his argument. He uses logical reasoning to explain the vast impact that plastic waste has on communities and the environment. He uses expressions of disgust and sadness accompanied by stories and images to describe the negative effect that mass consumerism has. Finally, he uses an optimistic tone to inspire the audience to take action. Although he does not identify the financial limitations of producing recycled plastic pellets, Mike Biddle successfully markets his company, the industry of recycled plastics, and the benefits of sustainability made good.

Work Cited

Biddle, Mike. "We Can Recycle Plastic." *TEDGlobal 2011*, 15 July 2011, Edinburgh, Scotland, www.ted.com. Accessed 12 Feb. 2018. Conference Presentation.

Solar Power

by Benton Reese

This planet is being drained of its resources at an alarming pace. Traditional fuels, such as coal, natural gas, and most of all oil, are no longer sustainable. The solar industry provides a welcome alternative to biofuels, but, in spite of its numerous benefits and public prominence, solar power, like many alternative fuels, has yet to become the panacea it was thought to be. While shifting away from fossil fuels is extremely crucial to the preservation of our planet and its inhabitants, the transition into the clean, renewable energy of solar power, although elegant on paper, seems to create more problems than it solves when applied practically. The United States, Saudi Arabia, and China are all seeking to make this transition, and each faces hurdles that are simultaneously unique and universal. The most prominent hurdles are the evolving job markets, personal inconvenience, and the lack of an international energy plan.

In the United States, employment rates have already been a major cause of concern, and the burgeoning solar industry has already begun to eclipse existing biofuel companies. One such example is the coal industry, in which "jobs have shrunk by forty percent since 2011," according to science writer and radio producer Reid Frazier. Frazier adds that "there are more than twice as many jobs in solar as in coal" (Frazier). At first glance, this job outlook may seem promising for those intending to start careers in the solar industry, but this still leaves many coal miners with specialized knowledge and trade skills with no alternative employment.

The availability of employment is not the only issue: money also plays a role in the discontent of modernizing workers: "If coal miners average about $35 an hour, for renewables it's more like $20 or $25" (Frazier).

While to some this may not seem like much, at its worst that is a difference of about $28,000 every year, bringing a coal miner's average annual income from around $67,000 to a mere $38,000. Rob Godby, an energy economist at the University of Wyoming, aptly states "that doesn't mean you couldn't raise a family on that, but you're a lot closer to the average income in a lot of states in the solar industry than you are in mining industries" (qtd. in Frazier). At a time when tension from an economic crisis is already heightened around America, few individuals would consciously decide to take a "50 to 70 percent pay cut" (Frazier). As the job market fluctuates, as it often does, it appears to the blue-collar worker currently employed by the biofuel industry that the only option is to learn a new trade in a newly developing industry, and accept less than the current standard of living.

But, as the job market changes, one thing stays the same: public opinion. As it is with every new technological development this side of the twentieth century, the shift toward solar energy has been met with dogmatic and obstinate resistance from the public, and nowhere is this more evident than in Saudi Arabia. As the chief exporter of oil in the world, Saudi Arabia is also the "sixth-largest consumer of oil," burning "about a quarter of the oil they produce"—a figure that has risen by seven percent every year (Ball 74). Despite the starkly apparent unsustainability in their practices, the Saudis continue to take their abundant energy for granted, and, according to British think tank Chatham House, "if this trend continues, domestic consumption could eat into Saudi oil exports by 2021 and render the kingdom a net oil *importer* by 2038" (74).

In light of these facts, what is keeping the Saudi people from making the shift to alternative energy? According to Jeffrey Ball, Stanford's scholar in residence at the Steyer-Taylor Center for Energy Policy and Finance, the most notable hindrances are the public's reliance on petroleum subsidies, "extensive social services funded by oil exports," and even the lack of a personal income tax imposed on its citizens (76). The Saudi Arabian government has begun the herculean task of shifting from a kingdom entrenched in oil to one stabilized by alternative energy, but, if they cannot gather support from a people motivated by a new desire for sustainability, the once proud Saudi Arabia could ultimately become dependent on those with better economic foresight.

It would appear that no other country has more economic foresight than China as they continue to build on the foundations of solar energy. With their excellent funding and superior manufacturing ability, China has even "eclipsed the leadership of the U.S. solar industry, which invented the technology, still holds many of the world's patents and led the industry for more than three decades," reports John Fialka, founding editor of *Climatewire* and former reporter for *The Wall Street Journal*. While the United States struggled to keep up with increasing demands for solar power, China had already started hiring experts, building massive factories, and buying and relocating existing solar companies. China's dominance of the world market has begun to put a significant dent in their United States competition, with three of this country's industry leaders already seeing a massive decrease in profits. Fialka notes that "SunEdison . . . filed for bankruptcy in April [2016]. The stocks of two other leading companies, First Solar and SunPower, [are] . . . floating between 13 and 6 percent of their former values." With this "monopolizing" of the solar industry, it is no surprise that "Liu Zhenya, former chairman of China's state-owned power company, State Grid Corp., came to the United Nations to shed more light on his nation's evolving solar ambitions, which he said are part of a plan aimed at organizing a global power grid that could transmit eighty percent renewable energy by 2050" (Fialka).

The plan has three phases: redesigning each nation's existing power grids to better support alternative energy, building regional grids capable of transmitting power across national borders, and building power lines and undersea cables to connect the regional grids. The idea is to "[generate] clean electricity in places like Africa and Central America that are among the richest when it comes to sunshine, and selling the clean energy to major cities that have the biggest need for it," thereby bringing income to these developing nations (Fialka). While these plans seem to herald a global transition to renewable energy, the primary obstacle is the unification of nations. Given its current trajectory, China will muscle out both the United States and Germany, former and current industry leaders respectively, and, with most of the profits subsequently funneling directly to China at the moment, there may be little incentive for cooperation in the future. While the U.N. meeting was attended by "representatives of 70 organizations, including government organizations, businesses and universities" (Fialka), given the current state of global upheaval coupled with the historical tendency toward discord and infighting, holding out for any sort of global cooperation effort in the near future may unfortunately be an exercise in futility.

With the threat of complete environmental expenditure constantly looming on the horizon, the glaring necessity for alternative energy becomes increasingly apparent. While it is clear that a vast spectrum of nations is hard at work in an attempt to present a united network of resources through which to develop solar technology and its production, there are still many obstacles to be overcome. In spite of these obstacles, more and more countries are pushing toward the future, and doing their part to create sustainable solutions and preserve our planet. After all, "the fact that Saudi Arabia, an ardent booster of fossil fuels, has found compelling economic reasons to bet on solar is one of the clearest signs yet that solar, at least in some cases, has become a cost-effective source of power" (Ball 77).

Works Cited

Ball, Jeffrey. "Why the Saudis Are Going Solar." *The Atlantic*, July/August 2015, pp. 72-80.

Fialka, John. "Why China Is Dominating the Solar Industry." *Scientific American*, 19 Dec. 2016, www.scientificamerican.com/article/why-china-is-dominating-the-solar-industry/. Accessed 3 Oct. 2017.

Frazier, Reid. "As Coal Jobs Decline, Solar Sector Shines." NPR, 6 May 2017, www.npr.org/2017/05/06/527047720/as-coal-jobs-decline-solar-sector-shines.

Part Two

SHINIER

Reshaping Elwood's World: How Elwood P. Dowd Reshapes His Life and Maintains Happiness in *Harvey*

by Caitlin Clausen

Upon taking a deeper look into the topic of Elwood P. Dowd's delusions in Mary Chase's play *Harvey* (1944) and the subsequent film of the same name (1950), specifically the creation of his imaginary friend Harvey, one may argue that Elwood has withdrawn from the world. It seems that he has isolated himself from having normal relationships because he spends an excessive amount of time with a human-sized rabbit. Elwood's sister Veta complains that she cannot live a normal life or find a husband for her daughter Myrtle Mae because Elwood's behavior scares people away. It seems as if Elwood has withdrawn from the world, but if one really examines Elwood's actions and dialogue, one can conclude that Elwood has not actually withdrawn from the world; instead, he has only reshaped his own world.

One factor that supports Elwood's reshaping of his world as opposed to withdrawing from the world is Elwood's statement to Dr. Chumley about a significant change in how Elwood had lived his life: "Years ago my mother used to say to me, she'd say, 'In this world, Elwood, you must be'—she always called me Elwood—'In this world, Elwood, you must be oh so smart, or oh so pleasant.' Well, for years, I was smart. I recommend pleasant. You may quote me" (Chase 7). This philosophy suggests to the audience that Elwood is an extremely intelligent man. He used to behave in a manner that convinced others that he was smart. Now, he does not care to impress others with his sharp mind and witty comments. Instead, he prefers to be pleasant. The way he speaks to people, flattering them and greeting them kindly, shows that he is a very warm and generous person. Elwood is very friendly and always treats the people whom he encounters with great respect. He has a positive and optimistic attitude, even when Dr. Chumley tells him that Elwood's sister Veta is trying to have Elwood committed to Dr. Chumley's mental institution. From this, one can conclude that Elwood is also very trusting, even when he should not be. He trusts both Veta's decision to have him committed and then her decision for him to receive Dr. Chumley's personality-changing serum. Most people would protest at being forced to take medication that would change a person's personality, but Elwood maintains his pleasant composure and agrees to have the procedure to keep his sister happy.

Another piece of evidence suggesting that Elwood has reshaped his world rather than withdrawing from the world is that he has invented an imaginary friend. His friend is a six-foot white rabbit named Harvey. Elwood and Harvey are very close; in fact, they go everywhere together. Wherever Elwood is, Harvey is almost always right there next to him. They go to bars and theatres together, walk around town together, and Harvey lives with Elwood. In the play, Dr. Simmons suggests that Elwood may have invented Harvey as a way of coping with Elwood's mother's death. It is possible that Elwood created an imaginary friend to comfort him during a difficult time of grieving. Most people cannot see Harvey, so Elwood appears to be insane when he is seen talking to himself and staring at an invisible being. Veta and her daughter Myrtle Mae are very distraught over Elwood's delusion because they feel that his strange behavior is affecting their social lives. They are embarrassed to invite guests to the home because they are ashamed of Elwood. On the other hand, Elwood remains quite content and cheerful. He is delighted to have the company of Harvey, who is such a special friend to him. He almost seems to be obsessed with Harvey. It is clear that Harvey is a source of comfort.

Elwood has reshaped his own life to fit Harvey into every situation, and this bond has made Elwood very happy since his first meeting Harvey on a street corner, a circumstance which might strike some as suggesting a stereotypically brief, physical encounter or "pick-up." Elwood's habit of frequently putting his arm around Harvey suggests that the relationship may very well be intimate in nature. In the 1940s, homosexual relationships were not socially acceptable. However, Elwood's going out for drinks with Harvey and to the theatre could lead one to believe that Harvey and Elwood have been "dating" and are now an established "couple," especially when Elwood brings home a double portrait of himself and Harvey. When Elwood realizes that Harvey is not staying at the institution to help Dr. Chumley but returning to the Dowd home, Elwood asks, "Was anything the matter? No—I—I thought you'd decided to stay with Dr. Chumley. You—you—huh? You-Well thanks, Harvey. I prefer you, too" (Chase 27). Elwood and Harvey clearly have a cherished bond with one another that leads one to believe that they are romantically involved, or at least that the relationship is one that would be seen as a traditional romantic relationship if Elwood and Harvey were a man and a woman.

Elwood does not spend much time with other friends—male or female; although, he is tremendously gracious and friendly to everyone. He often invites strangers over to his house for dinner or to the bar for drinks. What he does not do is spend time with other men and women without Harvey present. On the few occasions when Harvey is not present, Elwood speaks about him incessantly. Elwood has created a life that makes him happy and a partner who makes him happy, whether or not this partner is real does not matter to Elwood. Instead of withdrawing from a world that does not accept him, Elwood creates a world that he finds pleasant. This is not only a way of coping with a world that may seem boring, cold, or judgmental, but also a way for Elwood to find fulfillment and happiness within his own life.

Works Cited

Chase, Mary. *Harvey: Comedy in Three Acts*. 1944. Acting ed., Dramatists Play Service, 1971.

Harvey. Directed by Henry Koster, performances by Jimmy Stewart and Josephine Hull, screenplay by Mary Chase and Oscar Brodney, based on the play by Mary Chase, Universal, 1950.

The Workplace in *Our Miss Brooks*: Discerning Acceptable and Appropriate Behavior at Work

by Andrew Ford

There are certain standards and ethics that a workplace must uphold in order for it to be a safe, positive and productive environment for all employees. If employees and frequent visitors to a workplace feel comfortable going to work every day or being part of the workplace environment and the environment continues to foster that feeling, the quality of work getting done will be at its best. This type of environment is beneficial to all parties and spells success by any definition. However, this balance can be easily disrupted by inflated egos, power struggles, objectification, and other disruptive forces. In the 1956 film *Our Miss Brooks*, we see two very different workplaces, but both have some level of toxicity in the work culture that greatly affects the quality of these workplaces. Each situation has its own ailment, each situation shows how a toxic environment can present itself in many different ways, and each situation must be dealt with appropriately.

The first work environment the audience sees in *Our Miss Brooks* is Madison High School. The film's protagonist is Connie Brooks, an English teacher starting her first day at her new job at Madison. When she arrives at the school, we are immediately introduced to Biology teacher Phillip Boynton and the school's principal Osgood Conklin. Mr. Conklin is to blame for the first problem in Madison's culture: Conklin's militaristic approach to running a high school. Upon meeting Miss Brooks, he is very clear about both his own background and his expectations of faculty. It is also clear that he is disliked by many members of the staff as well as by many students. While the rigidity and strict discipline shown by Mr. Conklin probably worked well for him while in the military, this same demeanor does not translate well to a civilian, educational setting. His exertion of power is criticized by many around him, including the superintendent of schools. This criticism leads to Mr. Conklin deciding to run for election to the superintendent's seat, a decision which creates its own host of problems in the workplace.

Later in the film, when Mr. Conklin decides to run for office, he recruits Miss Brooks to be his campaign manager for the election. She is reluctant at first as she is busy with both teaching her classes and giving private tutelage to student Gary Nolan. Mr. Conklin, however, is able to convince her when he suggests that he would be tapping Phillip Boynton to receive a promotion upon a Conklin victory. This is all Miss Brooks needs to convince her to take the job because she knows that the promotion will come with a raise that will allow Mr. Boynton, after a long courtship, to buy a ring and propose to her. So, in addition to overly-oppressive school policies, the school is now afflicted with political positioning and relationship entanglements. The students are now involved in the election of Mr. Conklin simply because they no longer want him as their principal, and all attention in the school is put on the election instead of running an effective high school. As if the situation could not be any more toxic, Mr. Conklin then requests that Miss Brooks seek a campaign donation and support from Gary's father, the newspaper publisher Lawrence Nolan. This results in her spending a good bit of time with Mr. Nolan and second-guessing her relationship with Mr. Boynton. In one political action, Mr. Conklin sends the whole school into a frenzy around him. In his ambitious rush for political office, Mr. Conklin throws a monkey wrench into the relationship of two of his best teachers, thereby causing an enormous amount of tension and stress that should not be present in an effective workplace.

Another example of a potentially toxic workplace in the film is the newsroom run by Lawrence Nolan, publisher/editor of Madison's newspaper. When the audience is introduced to this workplace setting, everyone is fulfilling their duties diligently. Then, we witness a display not uncommon for a film of this era, but very problematic for today's audience. We see a beautiful woman enter the main area of the newsroom, and every male in the room immediately and deliberately stops what he is doing to follow her every movement. She is the new hire for the Miss Lonely Hearts column and apparently the only female employee at the newspaper. These male gazes continue to follow the new "Miss Lonely Hearts" as she walks back toward her office. In the scene, "Miss Lonely Hearts" must be aware of her allure and appears to be sophisticated enough in her own era to use it to her advantage. However, these men see women coworkers as potential romantic/sexual interests only rather than defining them as colleagues worthy of respect and consideration. Consequently and for comic effect, no newsroom work gets done in the 1956 world of *Our Miss Brooks* and such attitudes would be totally unacceptable in today's work environments where most female workers would prefer to complete their work in peace and be given attention on the basis of the merits of their work.

These workplace examples not only show us in what ways these environments fall short of being acceptable places of work, but also provide us with solutions to intolerable situations. If Mr. Conklin had been more open to compromising on some of his more draconian policies, the Madison High School work culture would have improved and he would have accomplished more as a rational principal than as a belligerent superintendent. The problem arises from his ego not being able to handle justifiable criticism, so he has to compensate for this by trying to attain a position where even fewer could question his authority. The fragile self-esteem of Madison High School's leader leads to Madison High being a less than desirable work environment. As for Mr. Nolan's newspaper, the audience sees a more culture-wide issue in play as the male employees appear foolish in their objectification of "Miss Lonely Hearts" in the Madison newsroom, but the culture's objectification of all women was nothing to laugh at. *Our Miss Brooks* is an instructive example of the trials and tribulations of working-class America that continues to give insight in how to improve American work culture.

Work Cited

Our Miss Brooks. Directed by Al Lewis, performances by Eve Arden, Gale Gordon, Don Porter, and Robert Rockwell, Warner Bros., 1956.

Some Live to Work, Others Work to Live: Work Values in Guy de Maupassant's "The Necklace"

by Crystal Kim

The many different elements that need to be factored into the decision-making process when looking for a job or career field seem to go unnoticed by many. Amy Lindgren's "Understanding Your Work Values is Key" highlights three major values: extrinsic, intrinsic, and lifestyle (H1). These work values can be applied in an evaluation of a fictional work. For example, in Guy de Maupassant's "The Necklace," the lifestyle values—living in a big city, living abroad (or vacationing), and spending time with family and friends—are reoccurring themes throughout the story, and, by the end of "The Necklace," these lifestyle values become luxuries Mathilde and Mr. Loisel can no longer afford.

"Living in a big city" and "living abroad" are listed as two of the lifestyle values in "Understanding Your Work Values is Key." These two lifestyle values are closely connected in Maupassant's "The Necklace." The city plays an important role in the story from the beginning. Although Mathilde lives a fairly comfortable life in Paris, she dreams of living in a different type of Paris. Mathilde desires a much more exquisite life filled with more excitement. She "daydreamed of large, silent anterooms, decorated with oriental tapestries . . . imagined large drawing rooms draped in the most expensive silks . . . dreamed of perfume of dainty private rooms . . . of expensive banquets with shining place settings . . . imagined a gourmet-prepared main course carried on the most exquisite trays" (Maupassant 7). On the other hand, Mr. Loisel possesses an entirely different dream from that of his wife. Mr. Loisel gives up the funds he had saved "to buy a shotgun for Sunday lark-hunts the next summer with a few friends in the Plain of Nanterre" (Maupassant 8). He ends up giving up his dream of a hunting holiday in the country to buy a dress for Mathilde to help her live out her fantasy at the party (Maupassant 8).

Even on the other side of the tracks, in the lives of the needy, the theme of the city is just as important. Without the large population of the city and its many classes divided by wealth and status, Mr. Loisel would be unable to make a living as well as make monthly payments to pay off the debt resulting from Mathilde's loss of Mrs. Forrestier's necklace. Again, Mr. Loisel relinquishes any possibility of achieving his once obtainable dream of a vacation in the country in order to repay loans for which "he compromised himself for the remainder of his days" (Maupassant 11). It is also in the city during a "stroll along the Champs-Elysées" when Mrs. Loisel has a fateful meeting with Mrs. Forrestier. In this unexpected encounter, Mathilde learns the supposed diamond necklace she borrowed from Mrs. Forrestier was merely costume jewelry with a measly price tag of five hundred francs compared to the real diamond replacement necklace costing thirty-six thousand francs (Maupassant 11-13). Before the loss of the necklace, both Mr. Loisel and Mathilde can hope that their dreams might come true, but, after the loss of the necklace, they know that their dreams are unobtainable.

The last value listed in "Understanding Your Work Values is Key" is "spending time with family and friends." Mathilde does not seem to have any real friends or close family as she is daydreaming alone rather than enjoying the company of others at the beginning of the story (Maupassant 7). However, once Mathilde discovers "the horrible life of the needy" (Maupassant 12), she loses any spare time she possibly had before to spend with family or friends. Mathilde's time for reading at the beginning of the story is, after the loss of the necklace and the dismissal of the maid, filled with "heavy housework, dirty kitchen jobs" (Maupassant 12). Mathilde also probably loses her only friend mentioned in the story—Mrs. Forrestier. Mrs. Forrestier is offended when Mathilde returns what Mrs. Forrestier believes is the original necklace several days after Mathilde borrowed it (Maupassant 11). Also, ten years later, when Mrs. Forrestier and Mathilde coincidentally run into each other one Sunday along the Champs-Elysées, Mrs. Forrestier does not even recognize Mathilde, which underscores how the two women have severed all contact with each other (Maupassant 12-13).

Not only does Mathilde lose time to spend alone or with friends, but she also loses the ability to spend time with her one and only family member throughout the story, which is Mr. Loisel, her husband. In the beginning of the story, Mathilde and Mr. Loisel are able to have dinner together, but, once they enter the "life of the needy" (Maupassant 12), Mr. and Mrs. Loisel's time is occupied with work. As mentioned before, Mrs. Loisel's time is occupied with housework, and Mr. Loisel "worked evenings to make fair copies of tradesmen's accounts, and late into the night he made copies at five cents a page" (Maupassant 12). Mathilde and Mr. Loisel lose both time together and the possibility of "spending time with family and friends" mentioned in the article "Understanding Your Work Values is Key" because of the loss of the necklace.

The elements of the lifestyle values (living in a big city, living abroad [vacationing], and spending time with family and friends) mentioned in the article "Understanding Your Work Values is Key" all become unobtainable, far-fetched dreams for Mr. and Mrs. Loisel. The dreams of Mathilde and Mr. Loisel that might once have been accessible become distant memories by the end of Guy de Maupassant's "The Necklace." Though Mathilde is living in a big city that provides opportunities for her husband's (over)work, she is living out a lifestyle vastly different from the exquisite lifestyle she dreamed about once upon a time. Mr. Loisel's idea of vacationing in the country later becomes a dream he can no longer afford, and both Mr. and Mrs. Loisel lose the free time they had before to spend with family, friends, and each other. Instead, by the end of the ten years, after Mr. Loisel pays off all the debt, Mathilde, now an old, rude woman, is left pondering about how "little a thing it takes to destroy you or save you" (Maupassant 12) and wondering about a lifestyle in which she had not lost the necklace on that fateful night.

Works Cited

Maupassant, Guy de. "The Necklace." 1884. Translated by Edgar V. Roberts. *Literature: An Introduction to Reading and Writing*, edited by Roberts and Robert Zweig, 6th compact ed., Pearson, 2015, pp. 7-13.

"Understanding Your Work Values Is Key." *Atlanta Journal-Constitution*, 26 Aug. 2018, p. H1.

Female Gothicism and Charlotte Perkins Gilman's "The Yellow Wallpaper"

by Jada Spencer

During the late eighteenth and early nineteenth centuries, women writers established their main themes: the roles for women in marriage, the inequalities women faced in society, and the different ways women were viewed by men and by themselves. Before Gothic literature evolved, the world was not widely exposed to either the radical idea that women desired changes in their day-to-day treatment or that women had objections to the societally and medically accepted procedures they had to endure regarding mental illnesses. Gothic literature is known for its revolutionary language, exquisite diction, supernatural forces, radical ideas, and social philosophies. Gothic literature is also known for its themes of "confinement and rebellion, forbidden desire and 'irrational' fear" (Johnson 522). Often the writings are imbued with ominous tones, internalized conflict(s), and symbols, all of which are used to emphasize the systematic oppression women had to endure. Symbols throughout the Female Gothic are regularly the cruxes of the stories, and they are generally applied to muffle the direct arguments women refrained from using in direct protest against patriarchal power. A prime example is the infamous yellow wallpaper in "The Yellow Wallpaper" (1892) by Charlotte Perkins Gilman, which, in response to societal expectations for women to be picture-perfect wives, is used to represent how trapped and oppressed woman felt during the nineteenth century.

The Female Gothic was a reaction to patriarchal society's restrictions on women's rights and other forms of oppression intended to limit female potential. In the introduction to the anthology *Female Gothic*, Juliann E.

Fleenor argues that the genre relays a sense of self-loathing, fear, wonder, and frustration in women "[towards their roles in] ... sexuality ... and procreation" (Fleenor 15), often in an attempt to show readers that men during the nineteenth century saw women as complete dichotomies of themselves—a species that often teetered on the patriarchal views of a good and bad wife/woman. The Gothic's testing of marriage roles, touching on social taboos, and pushing boundaries of the patriarchal perceptions of women and their mental stability in the nineteenth century are the main reasons why Gilman's short story "The Yellow Wallpaper" is the perfect example of a Victorian era piece of Female Gothic literature.

In 1913, Gilman revealed in an article in her magazine *The Forerunner* that she wrote the short story because she suffered from post-partum depression and her "treatments" were not helping her get better but were, in reality, harmful to her mental health and well-being. Gilman wrote the short story to protest the treatments women and men were receiving for "melancholia" or modern-day depression ("Why I Wrote 'The Yellow Wallpaper,'" 1403). The treatment, as stated in both the story and essay, was to "live as domestic a life as far as possible" (1403). Gilman also emphasizes that the treatment provided by her physician resulted in her nearly going mad, and, according to Fleenor in "The Gothic Prism: Charlotte Perkins Gilman's Gothic Stories and Her Autobiography," "female exclusion," or the denial of women's basic rights and the "imprisonment behind four walls," eventually drove women insane (230). Not only were the treatments provided by physicians a way to persuade women into believing that their "nervous diseases" were simply figments of their fragile imaginations, but they were also used to oppress women by making them feel as if they were wrong for feeling depressed and for neglecting their sole purpose to be proper wives. "The Yellow Wallpaper" is Gothic literature because of its capability to push the boundaries of marriage roles, its record of psychological deterioration, and its menacing, resonant yellow wallpaper.

In the story, the central gothic element is the yellow wallpaper, which radiates a sinister presence in the story and causes Jane's hallucinations both in the rented house's bedroom and on the estate's grounds. The wallpaper aids the development of the story's tone by creating an eerie atmosphere. Jane helps amplify the Female Gothic by allowing the woman trapped behind the wallpaper to suffer like women being held captive to treat their mental illnesses and by a husband's authority over them. The narrator's reaction to her hallucination's confinement is a drifting toward insanity, and she wishes that she could "jump out of the window" (Gilman 1402) in order to soothe her anger and annoyance with the woman trapped in the wallpaper. Jane's mental instability is triggered by the yellow wallpaper which causes her environment to become repressive and results in mental mayhem that begins to "[yoke] the intricacy of the interior environment to the collapse of effective written expression" (Betjemann 101). Jane begins to feel unable to perform her everyday tasks, and her final mental breakdown is the crux of the story. Jane locks herself in her room and begins to shout that she refuses to be stuck behind the wallpaper any longer. Gilman's character imprisons herself while rejecting a prison of treatments and confinement made by others.

The intensity and severity of this final scene create the perfect gothic image of darkness, irrationality, and rebellion, especially rebellion against traditional views of women with mental illnesses. The Gothic Literature movement allowed women a chance to express their views on specific situations in ways that they were not allowed to do in other literary forms. Gothic stories and novels were originally seen as extravagant vehicles to scare readers, but the genre became a platform for women to vocalize their oppressions and to begin to eliminate the problems they faced. Symbols incorporated throughout their literary works allowed women to protest societal oppression while keeping intricate plots centered and intense. Gilman's strong symbol of the yellow wallpaper allows her to convey her protest of the wrongful treatment of women with mental illnesses while also expanding the power of the Gothic genre.

Works Cited

Betjemann, Peter. "Eavesdropping with Charlotte Perkins Gilman: Fiction, Transcription, and the Ethics of Interior Design." *American Literary Realism*, vol. 46, no. 2, 2014, pp. 95-115.

Fleenor, Juliann E. "The Female Gothic." *Female Gothic*, edited by Fleenor, Eden, 1983, pp. 3-16.

—. "The Gothic Prism: Charlotte Perkins Gilman's Gothic Stories and Her Autobiography." *Female Gothic*, edited by Fleenor, Eden, 1983, pp. 227-41.

Gilman, Charlotte Perkins. "Why I Wrote 'The Yellow Wallpaper.'" 1913. *The Norton Anthology of Literature by Women: The Traditions in English*, edited by Sandra M. Gilbert and Susan Gubar, 3rd ed., vol. 1, Norton, 2007, pp. 1403-04. 2 vols.

—. "The Yellow Wallpaper." 1892. *The Norton Anthology of Literature by Women: The Traditions in English*, edited by Sandra M. Gilbert and Susan Gubar, 3rd ed., vol. 1, Norton, 2007, pp. 1392-1403. 2 vols.

Johnson, Greg. "Gilman's Gothic Allegory: Rage and Redemption in 'The Yellow Wallpaper.'" *Studies in Short Fiction*, vol. 26, no. 4, 1989, pp. 521-30.

Positive Flawed Decisions: Decision Making in *The Dick Van Dyke Show's* "The Curse of the Petrie People"

by Michelle Martin

The life-altering actions and choices a person makes are rightly regarded as the defining moments of that person's existence. In these instances, momentous decisions are unavoidable. Even the average person is faced with thousands of decisions every day. Given the importance of decision making to humans as a species, we often represent difficult or complex decisions in hypothetical situations that do not affect our own more mundane reality, such as in fictional scenarios (e.g. stories, plays, films, etc.), in order to give depth to an otherwise static character. In her weekly business advice column, Amy Lindgren provides a list of suggestions to improve one's ability to make a good decision when it comes to career issues. These suggestions can be used to evaluate any or all of the numerous decisions made by a fictional character.

An example of a defining decision in "The Curse of the Petrie People" (2 Feb. 1966) occurs when Laura Petrie, after accidentally destroying a piece of jewelry in a garbage disposal, decides to replace the "cursed" Petrie family heirloom that her mother-in-law Clara Petrie has just given her. The heirloom is a very large gold brooch shaped like the United States of America. The brooch features a small precious stone in the birth city of each male Petrie family and represents the entire Petrie clan. Unfortunately, a replacement brooch will probably not be ready in time for Laura to wear when Rob and Laura go out to dinner with Rob's parents, Frank and Clara. Amy Lindgren warns about this specific decision-making pitfall: "Not putting a timeline on the decision is the mistake that causes more harm than probably any other" (Lindgren

H2). She also states how "conversely, getting this [a timeline] right can smooth out nearly every other mistake."

When applying Lindgren's suggestion to the decision Laura Petrie makes in this episode of *The Dick Van Dyke Show* (1961-1966), one can see how Laura clearly does not lay out her timeline when making her "in the moment" decision to replace the brooch. This could represent her concern for her mother-in-law's approval and love; indeed, she cares about protecting the feelings of Clara so much that she does not think twice about replacing the brooch despite her time restraints. Mr. Marx, the jeweler who fashions a similar brooch to replace the original, mangled one, understands fear of a mother-in-law's disapproval as he fits replacing the brooch into his schedule, which alleviates Laura's timeline problem. If Mr. Marx had not understood the need for urgency, then Laura potentially could not have gotten the brooch replaced in coordination with her strict timeline. This is a classic example of situational irony as Laura's mistake, failure to put a realistic timeline on her decision, turns out to be a good choice in the long run.

One thing that Laura Petrie does correctly when making her choice to replace the "ugly" brooch is that she apprehends the decision-making process appropriately: "For decisions with long-term life impacts, it makes sense to put effort into the process [of decision making]" (H2). Living with the ever-increasing regret of *not* going to too much trouble to replace the brooch qualifies as a long-term life impact because Laura's accidental mangling of the brooch would exacerbate any other problems in her relationship with her in-laws. Another of Amy Lindgren's suggestions in her article is how not asking anyone for input before making a decision can be a mistake: "Not considering any other views can leave you vulnerable to gaps in logic or missed alternatives." Laura asks for advice from both her friend Milly and the jeweler Mr. Marx before following through with their suggestions in having a new brooch made. These aspects of Laura's decision to have a replacement brooch made clearly demonstrate that she successfully avoids a pitfall during her decision-making process.

Another example of an analyzable decision in "The Curse of the Petrie People" is Clara Petrie's sudden and surprising decision to forgive Laura. In one of the final scenes of the episode, after Laura confesses to destroying the Petrie brooch, Clara makes the choice to come clean about always hating the brooch and forgives Laura for accidentally destroying it. In making this decision, Clara "falls" into one of Amy Lindgren's pitfalls, called "acting on the rebound." Although this choice to forgive Laura turns out to be a good thing and most likely helps build their mother/daughter-in-law relationship into a stronger one, Clara Petrie does not think twice about immediately forgiving her son's wife and telling everyone the truth. This is an example of what should be a "decision-making pitfall" turning out to be a positive thing. If Clara had instead taken her time determining her course of action after finding out her brooch was gone, she may have come to a different conclusion and may have gotten mad at Laura. In that case, the whole episode would have ended with a different outcome and overall mood. Obviously, Clara forgiving Laura and bonding over the very real ugliness of the family brooch is both an unexpected and a comical development in the plot of this 1960s television show.

It is apparent that many factors go into making decisions, and even more go into avoiding making bad choices. In *The Dick Van Dyke Show*'s "The Curse of the Petrie People," both Laura and Clara make decisions that affect their relationship for the better. Laura decides to have the heirloom brooch replaced, thereby showing her desire to make her mother-in-law happy. Clara decides to forgive Laura and is thrilled to know that Laura has gone through the trouble of replacing the cumbersome brooch for the sake of the Petrie family. These decisions, although partly contrary to Amy Lindgren's strategies and partly consistent with them, are successful for both women. This is evidenced by the positive outcome that results at the end of this television show episode. By using Amy Lindgren's strategies to avoid decision-making pitfalls, one can evaluate decisions made by fictional characters.

Works Cited

"The Curse of the Petrie People." 2 Feb. 1966. *The Dick Van Dyke Show: The Complete Fifth Season*, performances by Dick Van Dyke and Mary Tyler Moore, episode 5, RJL Entertainment, 2014, disc 3. 5 discs.

Lindgren, Amy. "How To Avoid Decision-Making Pitfalls." *Atlanta Journal-Constitution*, 26 Jan. 2018, p. H2.

A Gladys Kravitz in Every Neighbor: Neighbors in William Faulkner's "A Rose for Emily" and Angela Robinson's *Professor Marston and the Wonder Women*

by Sofi Taher

In stories that involve a peculiar character or a peculiar relationship, there always seems to be a curious, annoying neighbor whose mission is to ferret out secrets. In the television situation comedy *Bewitched* (1964-1972), this neighbor is Gladys Kravitz, an intrusive presence whose snooping was developed through the run of the series by two talented comic actresses (i.e. Alice Pearce [1964-1966] and Sandra Gould [1966-1971]) (Abbott). Whenever a Gladys Kravitz-type character enters a situation, tension is created and, more often than not, what was meant to be kept secret is revealed. In William Faulkner's "A Rose for Emily" (1931), the main character Emily has very little to do with the town she lives in, but the townspeople are so nosey that they appear to act like her neighbors. In *Professor Marston and the Wonder Women*, director Angela Robinson deals with an uncommon family that includes Professor Marston, Elizabeth Marston, and Olive Byrne, all of whom encounter conflict in suburbia with their twentieth-century neighbors. Both neighbor situations, in the short story and the film, involve inquisitive, yet oblivious neighbors who are judgmental when it comes to romance in the lives of the main characters. All the protagonists, Emily Grierson and the Marston ménage, deal with unsavory neighbors, but the neighbors depicted in *Professor Marston and the Wonder Women* exhibit more hatred.

Curiosity is a trait shared by all the neighbors in both narratives, but their ignorance prevents them from quickly discovering the truth: Emily's hidden dead lover and Professor Marston's romantic relationship with two women. In "A Rose for Emily," curiosity is especially prominent at Emily's funeral: "When Miss Emily Grierson died, our whole town went to her funeral . . . the woman mostly out of curiosity to see the inside of her house" (Faulkner 96). Some years before her death, Emily is the subject of her neighbors' surveillance: "Now and then we would see her at a window for a moment, as the men did that night when they sprinkled the lime, but for almost six months she did not appear on the streets" (Faulkner 99). The townspeople intervene in her business, but ironically fail to recognize that she is damaged and hides a dead lover. Similarly, Professor Marston, Elizabeth Marston, and Olive Byrne encounter a curious neighbor. A neighbor walks in their house unannounced, and sees a nude Professor Marston bound to his costumed wife while a burlesque-attired Olive is pulling the ropes tight. This encounter takes place quite some time after the family moves into their suburban bliss with a cover story that Olive is a widowed mother of two. Consequently, the alias keeps the neighbors from being intrusive; therefore, they are oblivious at first to the unusual relationship.

The Jefferson townspeople and the Marston neighbors are very inquisitive about the romantic lives of Emily and Professor Marston, and this also leads them to being very judgmental. Faulkner explains the townspeople's negative perspective on Emily's romance: "At first we were glad that Miss Emily would have an interest, because the ladies all said, 'Of course a Grierson would not think seriously of a Northerner, a day laborer.' But there were still others, older people, who said that even grief could not cause a real lady to forget *noblesse oblige*, without calling it *noblesse oblige*" (98). This indicates that the townspeople make unjust assumptions about Emily because of her prominence and because she has a relationship with someone below her status. This relationship of unequals is incomprehensible to them during the post-Civil War era. For Professor Marston, the judgment begins in the scene when the neighbor walks in on the three having intercourse. At first, the scene is shot from the Marston ménage perspective which solely reveals romance, not the "abnormality" of a three-way relationship in suburbia during the 1940s. Later in this scene, however, the film's positive approach to the Marston ménage abruptly disappears with the nosy neighbor's entrance. To the intruding neighbor, this scene is not romantic but perverse. All of a sudden, a sexual scenario offering pleasure to its participants also looks a little ridiculous because of the unexpected judgement of an intrusive neighbor.

Although the two narratives have their similarities, the actions of the neighbors in the Marston situation are more intense. After the other neighbors find out about the Marston ménage, all of the Marston children are bullied. This leads to a fight between Professor Marston and a suburban father which creates even more drama in the family. Emily's situation is less intense because the neighbors discover her secret of a dead body after her death, which results not in violence but shocked silence. In addition, the audience's reaction to the two stories is different. For example, Ben Dickinson for *Elle* writes, "The ending of the movie provides a startling answer to the question of how genuinely multivalent were the relationship dynamics in the Marston household—and it will send you out of the theater with a huge grin on your face" (80). Faulkner's portrayal of Emily is judgmental in that Emily is never offered a chance to explain her actions; consequently, the audience is less sympathetic towards her and most rush to judge her as Homer's murderer.

Overall, the neighbors in "A Rose for Emily" and *Professor Marston and the Wonder Women* exhibit a great many similarities, but the differences are enhanced in *Professor Marston and the Wonder Women*, thereby creating a greater impact on the neighbors in the film and, through them, the film's audience. The film has a greater impact as it is a visual story, and this allows for more immediate impact than the written word. In the short story, Emily's character does not have the opportunity to show the audience her emotions and thoughts, thus allowing the audience to trust the neighbors' perspective more. The neighbors in both narratives demonstrate that there may be a little Gladys Kravitz in everyone. Viewers of the television series *Bewitched* thought that Gladys Kravitz was annoying, and her husband thought she was crazy, but Gladys is the only person observant enough to realize that something is different about the Stephens family. This mirrors how the townspeople feel toward Emily, and how the neighbors feel toward Professor Marston and his "wonder" women.

Works Cited

Abbott, Reginald. "English 1102 Television Handout." Perimeter College, Georgia State University, Dunwoody, Oct. 2017.

Dickinson, Ben. "Some Kind of Wonderful." Review of *Professor Marston and the Wonder Women. Elle*, Nov. 2017, p. 80.

Faulkner, William. "A Rose for Emily." 1931. *Literature: An Introduction to Reading and Writing*, edited by Edgar V. Roberts and Robert Zweig, 6th compact ed., Pearson, 2015, pp. 96–100.
Professor Marston and the Wonder Women. Directed by Angela Robinson, performances by Luke Evans, Rebecca Hall, and Bella Heathcote, Tara Theatre, Atlanta, 25 Oct. 2017.

Identity in Langston Hughes's *Mulatto* and Alice Walker's "Everyday Use"

by Hannah Huff

Socrates once said, "To know thyself is the beginning of wisdom." But what exactly makes you the person you are and me the person I am? Finding and understanding your own identity are vital steps toward achieving happiness in life. This phenomenon of knowing oneself is a topic often explored by authors who have either had trouble finding themselves or witnessed someone lacking self-knowledge. Since the enigma of understanding oneself is very common in everyday life, it became a subject for literary realism. Literary Realism is a movement that began in the nineteenth century and utilized the normal routines of life to express the significance of ordinary people. Even though the movement itself ended, the techniques used in realism continue to be important to literature.

Two works that use realism in unique ways are Langston Hughes' *Mulatto* (1935) and Alice Walker's "Everyday Use" (1973). *Mulatto* depicts Southern life in the 1930s and addresses the color line. Colonel Norwood is a plantation owner who lives with his black housekeeper Cora. The two have had five mixed children together, and four are still living. Conflict in this drama surrounds the youngest son Robert and his desire for community recognition and honor as the son of a white father. Walker's short story "Everyday Use" explores two different ways of celebrating and controlling African-American culture. Dee, who is seen as the antagonist by certain critics, visits her mother's house to see her mother and younger sister Maggie. Dee and Mama do not have a strong mother-daughter relationship, especially obvious when Dee forces education on her mother, a women who did not attend school after second grade. A conflict arises when Dee finds quilts made by her mother, aunt, and grandmother, and wishes to take them with her. Dee wants to put the quilts on display to celebrate freedom while Maggie would use them as quilts. In "Everyday Use," Walker critiques misinterpretations of the ideas expressed by black awareness groups in the 1960s and 1970s. A consideration of both the play and the short story reveals many similarities between the two. Both Hughes and Walker write in a realistic style to create the characters of Robert and Dee, characters who mirror one another by both being static and by experiencing an identity crisis. Robert and Dee are also used by Hughes and Walker to challenge those who attempt to deny their backgrounds.

Even though the play and the short story are almost forty years apart, the ways in which Hughes and Walker depict the settings are closely related. *Mulatto* was written before World War II. During the Great Depression, the unemployment rate for African-Americans was three times that of the white unemployment rate. Richard Barksdale, author of the critical essay "Miscegenation on Broadway: Hughes's *Mulatto* and Edward Sheldon's *The Ni**er*," points out that in 1935 "blacks in the South were still voteless, powerless, and legally segregated; and blacks in the North lived, in the main, in poverty-stricken ghettos" (192). African-Americans expressed their desires for change by heavily supporting the democratic candidates in the 1928 and 1932 presidential elections. In *Mulatto*, Hughes uses details accurate to the time when Higgins, a bromidic plantation owner and friend of Colonel Norwood, states, "All this post-war propaganda on the radio about freedom and democracy—why the ni**ers think its meant for them! And that Eleanor Roosevelt, she ought to been muzzled" (1356). Hughes also depicts sharecropping on a plantation in Georgia. These details add to the realism of the play as readers can put the situations in context with real occurrences in history.

"Everyday Use" was written in the early 1970s, a time referred to as the Post-Civil Rights Movement era. These years were aimed towards achieving the goals outlined in the 1960 reform movements. African-Americans looked towards finally being seen and wanted to control how their race was represented. Blacks celebrated their African roots and revived the positive aspects of their past to combat oppression. Different types of groups emerged to resist tyranny further; one of these groups was the Black Panther Party. Joe Sarnowski, author of "Destroying to Save: Idealism and Pragmatism in Alice Walker's 'Everyday Use,'" explains that Hakim-a-barber, Dee's boyfriend, represents a member of one of these groups as "his alliance with Black Islam seems to portray Hakim as idealistically-minded for that community's defiance of racism and promotion of African American independence and self-initiative" (271). This method of expressing pride in the black race is one that Dee favors. Along with parodic representations of these groups, Walker includes time-specific details. When Dee arrives at her mother's house and exits the car, "she peeks next with a Polaroid" (496). The Polaroid Land Camera gained popularity in the 1970s as it provided consumers with instant photographs minutes after being taken. Hughes and Walker use details relevant to the time periods like post-war propaganda and black Islam groups to blend historical context into their works smoothly.

In addition to the way in which historical context is presented, Hughes and Walker create similar static characters in *Mulatto* and "Everyday Use." Robert and Dee remain the same from the beginning to the end. Both maintain uppity personalities in which they believe their way of thinking is superior to their own families. Despite what anyone in his family says, Robert continues to live "resenting his blood and the circumstances of his birth" (1352). Robert is convinced that he should be able to choose to be treated like a white man because Colonel Norwood is in his blood. Germain Bienvenu in "Intracaste Prejudice in Langston Hughes's *Mulatto*" claims that, since Bert was a young boy, he "felt secure enough to proclaim his relationship to the most prominent white man in the area publicly" (342). While his siblings are grateful for what they have received from Norwood, Robert desires more, and he will not stop until he is granted what he wants, a father. Dee also remains fixated on her wishes for using the quilts. Instead of attempting to understand why Mama thinks Maggie is better suited for keeping the quilts, Dee begins to bash her little sister, "Maggie can't appreciate these quilts! She'd probably be backward enough to put them to everyday use" (498). Dee wants to use the quilts as a slap in the face to her "oppressors," her own family and their world. In "In Spite of It All: A Reading of Alice Walker's 'Everyday Use,'" Sam Whitsitt states that "what Dee also does is to denigrate in a more general sense the economic order of Mama's home and its system of values" (456). She feels that Mama is wasting treasures by promising them to Maggie. When Dee's wishes are not fulfilled, she leaves her mother's house with the same beliefs she had at her arrival. The fact that these characters refrain from change shows both how dedicated they are to their ideologies and how dismissive they are of others.

Finally, the two characters, Robert and Dee, offer new ways of approaching the meaning of heritage. The new approaches start when both rename themselves. When Robert first enters the play, he shouts, "Mister Norwood's here" (1360). Robert wants to pick and choose which parts of his heritage get to be expressed. He begins calling himself by his father's name to compensate for the nonexistent father-son relationship he has with Colonel Norwood. Robert's actions show that *Mulatto* focuses on "an aborted filial love" when "the black illegitimate son, in a scene of Oedipal fury slays his white father" (Barksdale 196). At this point, Robert's identity crisis is apparent. He has removed the man responsible for his misery from his life and is left unaware of what to do with himself. Since he rooted so much of his identity in the existence of Colonel Norwood, once Norwood is dead there is not much left to do but run and eventually take his own life to continue to have something over his father. In "Everyday Use," readers see that Dee's "new school" way of looking at heritage involves dismissing the ugly truths and parading the pretty aspects. She does not want to be reminded of where she came from unless it consists of an object that many would pay to see. Mama shows how dissatisfied Dee is with her upbringing when describing how their old house burned down, "Why don't you dance around the ashes? I'd wanted to ask her. She had hated the house that much" (495). Dee also takes part in renaming when she tells her mother she is now referred to as "Wangero Leewanika Kemanjo." What Mama sees as disrespect towards her family Dee sees as rebellion against her oppressors. Matthew Mullina in "Antagonized by the Text, Or, It Takes Two to Read Alice Walker's 'Everyday Use,'" claims that on this trip "Dee, now Wangero Leewanika Kemanjo, snaps Polaroids of her family house and establishes herself as a spectator to come to see her authentic roots" (41). She does not want to be included as part of her past. She only wants to explain how different she is from her past. Dee's identity crisis occurs when she is not understood by the people who are supposed to be closest to her, Mama and Maggie. After having the quilts snatched away from her, Dee sees how truly separate she is from her family and leaves her family home. She maintains her composure when she kisses Maggie before departing. Hughes and Walker use the actions of Robert and Dee to express unique, flawed interpretations of heritage.

Even though *Mulatto* and "Everyday Use" were written in two different time periods, the two works share similarities in the presentation of their main ideas and main characters. Both works involve struggling with identity and finding new meanings of heritage. Robert and Dee mirror one another by being static characters and maintaining the same desires from the beginning to the end. In the play and the short story, Robert and Dee may be seen as villains. Are they villains or just victims of the demands of society? Dee is not wrong when she says the name "Dee" comes from her oppressors. From her perspective, her oppressors include her own family. Robert also does not mean any harm by wanting a sense of closeness with his father; he simply deals with his inner conflict in a problematic way. Race is much more than something to select on a questionnaire. It can be a big part of people's lives, and differences in how race is expressed often lead to conflicts. These works also cause readers to question what exactly makes us family and what we are entitled to because of the circumstances of birth. Even though the story and the play do not end with favorable outcomes, the idea of finding one's own personal identity remains both a challenging and necessary human need.

Works Cited

Barksdale, Richard K. "Miscegenation on Broadway: Hughes's *Mulatto* and Edward Sheldon's *The N*gger.*" *Critical Essays on Langston Hughes*, edited by Edward J. Mullen, G. K. Hall, 1986, pp. 191–99.

Bienvenu, Germain J. "Intracaste Prejudice in Langston Hughes's *Mulatto*." *African American Review*, vol. 26, no. 2, Summer 1992, pp. 341–52.

Hughes, Langston. *Mulatto*. 1935. *Literature: An Introduction to Reading and Writing*, edited by Edgar V. Roberts and Robert Zweig, 6th compact ed., Pearson, 2015, pp. 1352–72.

Mullins, Matthew "Antagonized by the Text, Or, It Takes Two to Read Alice Walker's 'Everyday Use.'" *The Comparatist*, vol. 37, 2013, pp. 37–53.

Sarnowski, Joe. "Destroying to Save: Idealism and Pragmatism in Alice Walker's 'Everyday Use.'" *Papers on Language & Literature*, vol. 48, no. 3, Summer 2012, pp. 269–86.
Walker, Alice. "Everyday Use." 1973. *Literature: An Introduction to Reading and Writing,* edited by Edgar V. Roberts and Robert Zweig, 6th compact ed., Pearson, 2015, pp. 494–99.
Whitsitt, Sam. "In Spite of It All: A Reading of Alice Walker's 'Everyday Use.'" *African American Review*, vol. 34, no. 3, 2000, pp. 443–59.

A Chilling Resemblance: Emily Grierson in William Faulkner's "A Rose for Emily" and *Friday the 13th's* Jason Voorhees

by Jack Hardin

Mental illness has been a prominent theme in many classic horror stories from the past that are still well-known all across the United States. This is especially true in William Faulkner's chilling story "A Rose for Emily" (1931) where the development of a mental illness in Emily Grierson is what most likely prompts her to commit the heinous act of killing Homer Barron and keeping his corpse in her house. Although a lot less subtle than Faulkner's tale, another famous horror character shares the same homicidal impulse as Emily. In the film *Friday the 13th* (1980) directed by Sean Cunningham, the main antagonist Jason Voorhees becomes who he is as the result of both an inherited mental disability and a traumatic event that occurred in his childhood when he was thrown into a lake and left to drown. After he revives from drowning in the lake, he becomes the psychotic killer depicted in the film. Although these two killers seem entirely different, they share many characteristics that are shaped by the impact mental illness has on their lives. Both live most of their lives in isolation and cut themselves off from the outside world by not communicating with anyone, and they also feel as if they are both in positions of power by bending the rules or by making up their own.

Isolation from the rest of society is a key component to their madness. The narrator speaks of Emily like she is an outsider throughout the entire story. For most of her life, she is only with kinfolk, aside from the time she is with Homer Barron. She is described as "a tradition, a duty, and a care; a sort of hereditary obligation upon the town" (Faulkner 96).

She is not seen as a person who can be a friend; instead, she is seen as someone who is not so much human as legendary. This helps contribute to her isolation as it pushes her away from society and causes her to be in her own world. The same thing happens to Jason early on in his life. His mental disability deforms his body; consequently, children bully him. The people view him differently than they would a normal person, which diminishes his humanity. He is forced to separate himself from the rest of the world because of this rejection, which is what Emily ends up doing as well. Thus, both of their illnesses worsen and make them more likely to carry out their heinous acts. They also lack communication with the outside world because of their separation from society. For example, there are only a few instances in "A Rose for Emily" when Emily is seen interacting with people outside of her family and her home. When Jason begins his killing spree, he does not speak a word to anyone. It is likely that being alone for long periods of time with only their own thoughts leads to increased mental instability for both characters.

In both narratives, Emily and Jason demonstrate that they see themselves to be above the law. Emily displays this by choosing not to pay her taxes. Her father appears to have worked out a deal with the former mayor so that Mr. Grierson did not have to pay his taxes, and Emily assumes that this "tax free" status comes to her. Every time the tax collectors are sent to her home, she sends them back with no payment. This only contributes to her sense of power because the city never penalizes her for non-payment. She feels like she has the power to be able to control another human's life just as she controls the town, its laws, and its lawful representatives; thus, she kills Homer because she can without fear of punishment. On the other hand, Jason displays his sense of power by killing everyone who tries to open the camp where he was bullied when he was younger. He speaks through his mother at one point early on in the film and says, "Kill her, mommy! Kill her! Don't let her get away, mommy! Don't let her live!" Like Emily, Jason feels as if he has the power to take away someone else's life but the violent origins of this belief result in his much more violent methods of killing. Both of these famous characters feel as if they are allowed to make up their own rules and do whatever they wish. Although they share many of the same characteristics, they take different paths to get to there: Emily is secretive and focused; Jason is loud and violent.

Mental illness can be caused in a variety of ways. For Emily, she comes to be who she is over a period of time. After long periods of time in seclusion, her mental illness develops behind a veneer of coexistence with a world whose manners and rules of inheritance and decorum she knows and uses to her advantage. For Jason, a violent, traumatic event is the catalyst for exacerbating his congenital mental illness. He does not show signs of becoming a psychotic killer early on in his life, and it takes children bullying him and throwing him into a lake to activate that side of him. Even though they get to be who they are in different ways, the end result is the same. They both turn into killers who seemingly feel no remorse for their actions.

Although they seem like two entirely different people, Jason and Emily share many chilling similarities. They are both deeply affected by a mental illness that causes them to commit their horrifying actions. Through this illness, they isolate themselves from society that further sends them into madness and also makes them begin to believe that they make the rules and they get to decide who is to live and who is not. In an era when the use of mental illnesses in horror stories is incredibly popular, the stories of these two fictional characters are so similarly chilling that they stand as standards for the rest.

Works Cited

Faulkner, William. "A Rose for Emily." 1931. *Literature: An Introduction to Reading and Writing,* edited by Edgar V. Roberts and Robert Zweig, 6th compact ed., Pearson, 2015, pp. 96–101.

Friday the 13th. Directed by Sean S. Cunningham, performances by Betsy Palmer and Adrienne King, Paramount Pictures, 1980.

Part Three

SHINIEST

The Dakota Access Pipeline: Human Beings Are More Important Than the Economy

by Isabella Coty

Native Americans have a history of being invisible to others who feel as if they have the right to take their land, almost as if they do not exist. Native Americans have been forced into one-sided treaties that gave the Europeans the better deal, or they have been attacked after refusing. Since the moment Christopher Columbus stepped onto American soil, Native Americans have been seen as inferior. In Columbus's journal, his first thought about the Native Americans was, "It appears to me, that the people are ingenious, and would be good servants" (Columbus). The fight over the Dakota Access Pipeline is a modern-day version of Native Americans being walked over and pushed to the side. Native Americans, along with other protesters, are putting their lives on the line to prevent the Dakota Access Pipeline from being put on their sacred land and potentially leaking into the Missouri River. A leak into that river would affect many millions of people. Furthermore, the Dakota Access Pipeline was not originally on Native American land: it was moved south because of North Dakota's refusal to let it continue through its territory (Thorbecke). Protesters who signed a petition on *CredoAction.com* believe that "the Dakota Access pipeline would fuel climate change, cause untold damage to the environment, and significantly disturb sacred lands and the way of life for Native Americans in the upper Midwest" (Yan). However, Energy Transfer Partners, who is in charge of the installation of the Dakota Access Pipeline, believes that the pipeline is an efficient way to safely transport oil, and is continuing to build it despite widespread resistance. Although there may be benefits to the Dakota Access Pipeline, it should not be built because it is a terrible threat to the environment, places economic interests above human interests, and is an immoral violation of Native American sovereignty.

It has been claimed that the Dakota Access Pipeline is a safe way to transport oil. The Transportation Safety Board reports that "73 per cent of pipeline occurrences result in spills of less than 1m^3, and 16% of occurrences result in no spill whatsoever" (Green and Jackson). Pipeline accidents usually do not impact the environment, and pipelines as a mode of oil transport have fewer spills than other methods. This makes the pipeline the safest way to transport crude oil. Additionally, Energy Transfer Partners states that the "Dakota Access will be built and operated using the most advanced technology and monitoring systems to make it even safer." The Dakota Access Pipeline technology will exceed the federal safety standard. The Energy Transfer Partners will look at the pipe and use an x-ray to inspect each individual weld ("Dakota Access Pipeline Facts"). The pipeline will be monitored round-the-clock, and it can be shut down if needed. Further, the Dakota Access Pipeline will lessen the reliance on rail and truck transportation to move crude oil, which is better for the environment because there are more rail and truck accidents when transporting oil than when using pipelines. Trains can explode and cause major disasters, while most pipeline leaks are small in comparison. The Dakota Access Pipeline allows crude oil to be transported in the safest way, which is better for the environment.

However, The Dakota Access Pipeline is a terrible threat to the environment and it has the potential to do drastic harm. The risks need to be taken into account and weighed against the benefits of the pipeline. Tony Keller of *The Globe* writes, "If the pipelines are built, then that oil will be taken out of the ground, refined and burned, with significant greenhouse-gas emissions," which means greenhouse gases will be emitted indefinitely. Lyndsey Gilpin further notes that the Dakota Access Pipeline will cause fungus and microbes if, during installation, equipment is not handled right. In addition, the pipeline has the potential to harm endangered species' habitats by destroying them when excavating for the pipeline. If a leak were to happen, many endangered water birds could be negatively affected. In the article "How Oil Affects

Birds," readers learn that a leak could make these animals' ecosystems unlivable, which would lead to deaths because birds will be exposed to oily water and would not be able to escape ("How Oil Affects Birds"). Finally, the biggest problem of the Dakota Access Pipeline is that it could threaten drinking water from the Missouri River, which would affect millions of people. The Dakota Access Pipeline may have benefits, but the repercussions on the environment, along with the risk of a leak, are too serious to ignore.

Energy Transfer Partners, however, claimed that the Dakota Access Pipeline will help to improve local and national economies. The pipeline will create thousands of jobs in construction, engineering, mechanics, and more. It will reduce rail transportation, leaving more available rail cars for agriculture ("Dakota Access Pipeline Facts"). Communities along the Dakota Access Pipeline route could see an increase in hotels, restaurants, and other services being used, which is good for local business. Even more, it has been claimed that the pipeline would allow the United States to be less reliant on foreign countries for oil, which would be safer and less expensive. Energy Transfer Partners says that "every barrel of oil produced in the United States directly displaces a barrel of foreign oil," which is good because relying on another country for something as important as oil is problematic. The Dakota Access Pipeline would bring millions of dollars in property, income, and sales taxes, which will be used to benefit local communities by supporting schools, roads, and emergency services ("Dakota Access Pipeline Facts"). The Dakota Access Pipeline would help the United States to become more self-sufficient in producing oil and would help the economy in a huge way.

Nevertheless, opponents of the Dakota Access Pipeline maintain that the pipeline will put the economy over the environment and the human beings of the Standing Rock Sioux Tribe. It would even negatively affect the Standing Rock Sioux Tribe's economy because, while the pipeline construction is happening, many tribe members are not able to continue with their daily jobs, and this is economically dangerous for the whole tribe. Also, the tribe will not benefit from the economic gains in the same way the rest of South Dakota will because the pipeline will pay them nothing, while other landowners will be paid for giving up land. The benefits from increased use of hotels, motels, and restaurants for people connected to Energy Transfer Partners are not something that would be profitable for Native Americans. The tribe is also very poor; for example, Alicia Adamczyk states in "The Dakota Pipeline Could Devastate Some of the Poorest People in America" that "more than 40% of the reservation's population has an income below the federal poverty line." If the pipeline were to leak into the Missouri River, the tribe's farming and cattle businesses would be in danger. This would be a huge problem because these businesses provide most of their economy. The Standing Rock Sioux Tribe will suffer economically if the Dakota Access Pipeline is built.

Significantly, the biggest problem has been that Energy Transfer Partners believes they have the right to build the Dakota Access Pipeline on the proposed route, but the Native Americans claim the plan is an immoral violation of Native American sovereignty. Energy Transfer Partners has bought surrounding land for the Dakota Access Pipeline from landowners. The Midwest Alliance for Infrastructure Now confirmed that all landowners in North Dakota have approved the construction on their land (Yan). Energy Transfer Partners claims the pipeline does not cross into the Standing Rock Sioux Tribe's land and that the land they are building on is outside of the reservation. In addition, Energy Transfer Partners claims that the pipe cannot be rerouted without extreme consequences, such as having to pay millions of dollars, and part of the pipeline is already built. Delaying the Dakota Access Pipeline would also harm Energy Transfer Partners because millions of dollars are being lost from not being able to produce the oil on time. Energy Transfer Partners believes they have done all they are capable of doing to acquire the land needed for the Dakota Access Pipeline.

On the contrary, the Standing Rock Sioux Tribe claims that they were not consulted about construction on their land, and that the tribe owns land Energy Transfer Partners wants to build on. The tribe has said that the Dakota Access Pipeline will destroy their tribal burial and prayer sites. The Dakota Access Pipeline was not approved by the Standing Rock Sioux Tribe; they were not consulted about where the Dakota Access Pipeline could be built (Hult). The Standing Rock Chairman, David Archambault II, commented that "His tribe will settle for nothing less than stopping the pipeline's construction" (Yan). The construction workers and private security do not even have the right to be on the Standing Rock Sioux Tribe's land according to the Laramie treaty, which allows the Native Americans to have control over who enters their land (Herold). Energy Transfer Partners claims that they own the land are false because the Dakota Access Pipeline goes on the edge of the Standing Rock Sioux Tribe's territory.

In sum, the Dakota Access Pipeline should not be built. It has the potential to harm the surrounding environment and people. The Dakota Access Pipeline may bring about a safer way to transport oil, but the consequences are too risky; the route falls onto Native American land. The pipeline would negatively affect the Native Americans, and it is immoral to take land from a group of people who have had their land stolen time and time again. In addition, the construction of the Dakota Access Pipeline should be rerouted and rechecked to see if it is worth the risk of building it under a major freshwater source, the Missouri River. Overall, it would be corrupt to build the Dakota Access Pipeline, and it would be a mistake for Energy Transfer Partners to risk an oil spill for money.

Works Cited

Adamczyk, Alicia. "The Dakota Pipeline Could Devastate Some of the Poorest People in America." *Money*, Time, 2 Nov. 2016, time.com/money/4551726/dakota-access-pipeline-standing-rock-sioux-tribe-devastate-poorest-people/.

Columbus, Christopher. "The Journal of Christopher Columbus (1492)." *Historyguide*, The History Guide, 1492, www.historyguide.org/earlymod/columbus.html.

"Dakota Access Pipeline Facts." *Dakota Access Pipeline Facts*, Energy Transfer, 2015, www.daplpipelinefacts.com/.

Gilpin, Lyndsey. "These Maps Help Fill the Gaps on the Dakota Access Pipeline." *High Country News*, 5 Nov. 2016, www.hcn.org/articles/these-maps-fill-the-gap-in-information-about-the-dakota-access-pipeline.

Green, Kenneth P., and Taylor Jackson. "Pipelines Are the Safest Way to Transport Oil and Gas." *Fraser Institute*, National Post, www.fraserinstitute.org/article/pipelines-are-safest-way-transport-oil-and-gas.

Herold, Kiana. "Terra Nullius and the History of Broken Treaties at Standing Rock." *Truthout*, Intercontinental Cry Magazine, 21 Nov.

2016, www.truth-out.org/news/item/38399-terra-nullius-and-the-history-of-broken-treaties-at-standing-rock.
"How Oil Affects Birds." *International Bird Rescue*, International Bird Rescue, www.bird-rescue.org/our-work/research-and-education/how-oil-affects-birds.aspx.
Hult, John. "4 Ways the Dakota Access Pipeline Could Be Stopped." *USA Today*, Gannett Satellite Information Network, 5 Nov. 2016, www.usatoday.com/story/news/nation-now/2016/11/05/dakota-access-pipeline-analysis/93362756/.
Keller, Tony. "Yes, Pipelines Increase Greenhouse Gases. Will Acknowledging It Kneecap Canada's Oil Industry?" *The Globe and Mail*, The Globe and Mail, 30 Mar. 2016, www.theglobeandmail.com/opinion/yes-pipelines-increase-greenhouse-gases-will-acknowledging-it-kneecap-canadas-oil-industry/article28434293/.
Thorbecke, Catherine. "Why a Previously Proposed Route for the Dakota Access Pipeline Was Rejected." *AbcNews*, 3 Nov. 2016, abcnews.go.com/US/previously-proposed-route-dakota-access-pipeline-rejected/story?id=43274356.
Yan, Holly. "Dakota Access Pipeline: What's at Stake?" *CNN*, Cable News Network, 28 Oct. 2016, www.cnn.com/2016/09/07/us/dakota-access-pipeline-visual-guide/.

A Home For Ninety Days: Addressing Homeless Families in America

by Emily Fritts

Anna, a single mother with two sons, will spend the morning packing up their car with the few things that they own and drive to a new host church or synagogue. It is Sunday, also known as moving day. They are set up in a ninety-day program called Family Promise. It is a national organization that dedicates its resources to aid homeless families in America from being separated in the traditional shelter system. Although Atlanta has many homeless shelters for men and women, communities throughout the city should support family shelters, because they stabilize the foundation of the family unit, protect the psychological well-being of children and provide resources to help families start over.

For many individuals in the United States, the thought of living without a home is unimaginable. However, for those who are without a home, having a stable support group is vital to the family's well-being. Anna emphasized the importance of having her children being able to stay with her during this difficult time. Though she did not feel comfortable sharing how long she had been without a home and in what cities she had been, she shared how her family had been turned away from other shelters. This occurred because her son was fifteen. Anna went on to explain that "in women's shelters, mothers and their children can stay there, but if the son is older than twelve, he has to go to a men's shelter. That is not right. It is not a safe place for a child. And that is my son, my child. He should be with me" (Anna). That is where Family Promise comes in to help.

The mission of Family Promise, started in New Jersey by Karen Olson in 1986, is to "help homeless and low-income families achieve sustainable independence through a community-based response" (*Family Promise*). In 1982, Karen was on her way to a meeting when she passed a homeless woman on the streets. On impulse, she decided to buy the woman a sandwich, which led to a conversation. Olson learned that homelessness was occurring in her suburban city of New Jersey. Fueled by this new information, she worked to build a network of various religious communities that would provide shelter, meals, transportation, and showers. The first official inter-faith hospitality network opened on 27 October 1986, in Olson's home state of New Jersey, and grew into a nationwide network. Today, Family Promise has helped over 67,000 people in need annually and has called over 180,000 volunteers to action (*Family Promise*). They have built a support group that holds families together and nurtures the growth of their children.

Being homeless affects all people involved, but it makes a substantial mental impact on adolescents. For families, having the ability to stay together ensures that children have the least traumatic experience during homelessness. Gerald Aldridge, Board Chair of Family Promise of North Fulton/DeKalb, commented, "One time there was a young girl, about six years old, who said that she didn't even know that they were homeless. That is how good this program is" (Aldridge). This program is unique, as it is truly able to care about its clients. Anna opened up about her youngest son's struggle with being homeless. At eleven, he struggles to find his place among children his age, and he has a low self-esteem. This has led him to look for friends in the wrong places. She went on to add that it is tough for him because he does not have a home to have people come over to do homework or have study groups. He feels uncomfortable going to other people's houses because he does not have one. She thinks that it is harder for him because he is younger and does not understand what is happening and why. However, she is thankful that they can stay together and that she can guide him through his problems and answer his questions. Though it is still a difficult situation to be in, having a community-based program lessens the stress and trauma that could threaten the psychological well-being of children.

Some may argue that this program is inefficient and does not provide for enough families. The general claim is that gender-specific shelters could improve efforts to accommodate families, such as family floors where they can sleep. The problem with this fix is that it does not give families space nor the help that they need to rear their children. As mentioned earlier, Anna talked about how men and women's shelters could accommodate for families, but the problem occurs when sons get older and cannot stay in women's shelters. Along with the age rule, she said that typical shelters also hinder a parent's authority and ability to move their family into transitional housing. Supporting Anna's claim is a study conducted at Florida State University which found that "living in a homeless shelter can exacerbate parental stress, because . . . shelter life may impose rules that undermine a parent's authority" (Holtrop, McNeil, and McWey). Living in the traditional shelter system not only takes away the privacy a family has but also drives away the parent's authority to choose how they rear their children. Beth Underhill, a board member at St. Luke's Presbyterian, talked about how families in the traditional shelter systems will have more trouble being present for their children, compared to living in a family-based shelter. They may suffer from stress, depression, substance abuse disorders and PTSD (Underhill). However, Family Promise has resources that are dedicated to meeting the specific needs of families with children so they can move on.

The ultimate goal of Family Promise is to move families from being homeless to living in transitional housing in ninety days. To achieve that goal, the Family Promise organization has equipped each community with a social worker and resources, such as computers, help with resume writing, and classes in interview skills. Gerald Aldridge describes the process, "Once a family is cleared to enter the program, they will be assisted in receiving free childcare that will allow them to look for jobs without that expense" (Aldridge). Receiving free childcare gives parents the independence to job hunt with ease, and allows them to save the money for a house to rent when they graduate from the program. Amy Donley of Florida State University discusses some factors that also help families escape homelessness, "families that successfully escaped homelessness . . . had more resources including a car and somewhat better incomes" (Donley et al.). Consequently, Family Promise prefers to take clients with cars because they grant more independence for the client to move throughout the program. Family Promise also works with clients to assist them in creating a budget to save money and works to provide the resources to increase income to push them into transitional housing. The significant benefit of a community-based organization is the generosity of volunteers who donate their time, skills, and resources to help families get back on their feet.

Thanks to the generosity of communities, the incredible work of Karen Olsen, and compassion that volunteers have for people in need, families have been able to find support, psychological security, and resources to recover their footing and dignity. Anna said, "Home is where the heart is. We didn't have a home, but we still had each other. We didn't have a home, but we had faith. We didn't have a home, but we had joy and peace and contentment" (Anna). She is right. No matter how hard or treacherous the road may be, family is forever the best home.

Works Cited

Aldridge, Gerald. Personal interview. 1 Nov. 2017.

Anna. Personal interview. 22 Oct. 2017.

Donley, Amy, et al. "How Stable Is the Condition of Family Homelessness?." *Society*, vol. 54, no. 1, Feb. 2017, pp. 46–55. *MasterFILE Elite*, doi:10.1007/s12115-016-0099-0. Accessed 22 Oct. 2017.

Family Promise, 2016, www.familypromise.org/who-we-are/. Accessed 22 Oct. 2017.

Holtrop, Kendal, Sharde McNeil, and Lenore M. McWey. "'It's a Struggle[, B]ut I Can Do It. I'm Doing It for Me and My Kids': The Psychosocial Characteristics and Life Experiences of At-Risk Homeless Parents in Transitional Housing." *Journal of Marital & Family Therapy*, vol. 41, no. 2, Apr. 2015, pp. 177–91. *Education Source*, doi:10.1111/jmft.12050. Accessed 22 Oct. 2017.

Underhill, Beth. Personal Interview. 15 Oct. 2017.

The Right To Choose Is the Right Choice

by Audrey Hewett

One would think that in a time of exponentially growing technology, abortion rates would be increasing, but, because of state government intervention, they have been decreasing. According to the Guttmacher Institute, in 2014, the U.S abortion rate hit an all-time low of 14.3%; the abortion rate of the year that abortion was legalized (1973) was 16.3%, which was higher than it is now. Although this rate is low, approximately one in four women in the United States will have an abortion in her lifetime (Guttmacher Institute). The heated debate on whether or not a woman should be able to get an abortion has become a very contentious topic within our nation; however, an even bigger issue has arisen from this debate—whether federal or state governments should regulate abortions. Some argue that only the federal government of the United States should create abortion legislation, but others counter that state and local governments have the authority to create their own abortion laws. Because it is deemed unconstitutional and creates immense inequality among women in different socioeconomic groups, state and local governments of the United States should not create any sort of legislation that may prevent a woman from obtaining an abortion.

Any state or local government legislation that restricts abortion in any way is deemed unconstitutional. Beginning with the landmark case of *Roe v. Wade* (1971), the Supreme Court of the United States of America has ruled that it is legal for women to get an abortion under the 14th Amendment. Prior to this Supreme Court ruling, "44 states outlawed abortion in nearly all situations that did not threaten the life or health of the mother" (Kliff). This case decided that "abortion fell within the right to privacy" and crucially "affected laws in 46 states" ("*Roe v. Wade* Fast Facts," 2017). After the ruling, abortions began to increase; however, abortion rates have recently decreased considerably because of several states' growing abortion regulations, regulations that are unconstitutional under the *Roe v. Wade* ruling. An example of these recent state abortion regulations is a new law created by the state of Texas in November of 2013. This legislation, House Bill 2, "required all Texas facilities performing abortions to meet hospital-like standards—which include minimum sizes for rooms and doorways, pipelines for anesthesia" (Ura). This caused "the number of facilities providing abortions," especially small, rural facilities, to decrease excessively, and "the number of medication abortions decreased by 70%" in comparison to the year before the law was implemented (Baum et al.). This made it extremely difficult for women to obtain an abortion in Texas, mainly those women who lived in non-urban areas of Texas. Because of its unconstitutionality, on 27 June 2016, this regulation was overturned by the Supreme Court of the United States. This legislation is one of many examples that prove that laws made by local governments to hinder a woman's ability to obtain an abortion are unconstitutional.

Another way that state regulations can be deemed unconstitutional is women, in some states, are denied abortions for religious reasons. Even though the United States of America is supposed to be a secular state, there are still state legislatures that, for underlying religious reasons, deny women the right to obtain an abortion and/or incriminate women for obtaining an abortion. In 2011, Nancy Hass of *Newsweek* described a case in which a woman, Jennie Linn McCormack, was arrested in the state of Idaho for inducing her own abortion. According to Hass, "Idaho has a 1972 law—never before enforced—making it a crime punishable by five years in prison for a woman to induce her own abortion." Idaho is also a state with the second highest population, about 26% (Cotterell), of followers of the Church of Jesus Christ of Latter-day Saints (Mormons). This religious group teaches that "elective abortion for personal or social convenience is contrary to the will and the commandments of God," and "therefore, the church says, any facilitation of or support for this kind of abortion warrants excommunication from the church" (Liu). This information ties the odd, 1972 Idaho law to the religious practice of Latter-day Saints, and proves that it is an outdated law with underlying religious background. Therefore, legislation like this is obsolete and proves that state and local governments of the United States should not regulate how a woman may obtain an abortion.

Furthermore, state and local government legislation restricting abortion creates immense inequality among women in different socioeconomic groups. As stated earlier, the Texas legislation of November 2013 shut down many facilities that provided abortion procedures—including many rural facilities. This made it extremely difficult for poorer women living in the rural areas of Texas to be able to obtain an abortion. Only a few select urban facilities were still open, so most women located in rural Texas could not find facilities that performed abortions near them. These women would have had to travel to urban cities in order to obtain an abortion legally, and most did not even have enough money to travel these great distances. On top of that, these women would then have to pay for the procedure itself. The combination of travel and procedure costs was too great for these women. In fact, some "women found the process of finding or getting to a clinic so onerous that they considered not having the procedure" (Baum et al.). In the case of Jennie Linn McCormack in Idaho, McCormack gave herself an abortion "out of desperation." According to *Slate*'s Mark Joseph Stern, for McCormack, "there were no abortion clinics anywhere in southeast Idaho, and an abortion in Salt Lake City, 138 miles away, could cost $2,000." These kinds of laws that make it much more difficult for women of lower socioeconomic groups to obtain abortions completely go against the 14th Amendment (Equal Protection Clause) that protects abortion in the United States of America:

> All persons born or naturalized in the United States, and subject to the jurisdiction thereof, are citizens of the United States and of the State wherein they reside. No State shall make or enforce any law which shall abridge the privileges or immunities of citizens of the United States; nor shall any State deprive any person of life, liberty, or property, without due process of law; *nor deny to any person within its jurisdiction the equal protection of the laws.*" (US Const. amend XIV, sec. 1; emphasis added).

Because abortion is protected under this amendment, including the rights of women in lower-class socioeconomic groups, restrictive state legislative actions are unconstitutional and should be overturned. Typically, lower-class women are those who need abortion rights the most. Some poorer women do not have the money to support themselves, let alone another human being. In some cases, these lower-class women already have a child or other children, so having another child could possibly cause the other children to suffer because of a lack of resources. And, for some women, having a child would interfere with her work. This could very possibly hinder a woman's health or standard of living if work is her only source of money to support herself.

State and local legislation that hinders a woman from obtaining an abortion is unconstitutional and creates immense inequality among women in different socioeconomic groups. These laws should be overturned, and all state and local governments should be prevented from creating any future restrictive legislation. Thorough research on this topic supports the proposition that any woman should be able to get an abortion, and legislation created by state and local governments should never be able to stop a woman from so doing if that is her choice. A woman should be able to control her own body, including whether or not she wants to give birth to a child. The ability of anyone to control their own body is a basic human right; it is not acceptable for the government to take away a woman's right to choose. Abortion is a right, not a privilege.

Works Cited

Baum, Sarah E., et al. "Women's Experience Obtaining Abortion Care in Texas After Implementation of Restrictive Abortion Laws: A Qualitative Study." *PLOS ONE*, vol. 11, no. 10, 26 Oct. 2016, pp. 1–14. EBSCO*host*, doi:10.1371/journal.pone.0165048.

Constitution of the United States.

Cotterell, Adam. "Why The Mormon Church Is Sending So Many Missionaries To Idaho." *Boise State Public Radio*, boisestatepublicradio.org/post/why-mormonchurch-sending-so-many-missionaries-idaho#stream/0.

Hass, Nancy. "The Next Roe V. Wade?." *Newsweek*, 19 Dec. 2011, pp. 25–27. EBSCO*host*,ezproxy.gsu.edu/login?url=http://search.ebscohost.com/login.aspx?direct=true&db=a9h&AN=69707769&site=ehost-live&scope=site.

"Induced Abortion in the United States." *Guttmacher Institute*, 20 Oct. 2017, www.guttmacher.org/fact-sheet/induced-abortion-united-states.

Kliff, Sarah. "CHARTS: How Roe v. Wade Changed Abortion Rights." *The Washington Post*, 22 Jan. 2013, www.washingtonpost.com/news/wonk/wp/2013/01/22/charts-how-roe-v-wade-changed-abortion-rights/?utm_term=.41116aa43fbc.

Liu, Joseph. "Religious Groups' Official Positions on Abortion." *Pew Research Center's Religion & Public Life Project*, 15 Jan. 2013, www.pewforum.org/2013/01/16/religious-groups-official-positions-on-abortion/.

"*Roe v. Wade* Fast Facts." *CNN*, 23 Apr. 2017, www.cnn.com/2013/11/04/us/roe-v-wade-fast facts/index.html.

Stern, Mark Joseph. "Idaho Woman Confounds Pro-Lifers' Legal Reasoning by Giving Herself an Abortion." *Slate*, 5 June 2015, www.slate.com/articles/double_x/doublex/2015/06/jennie_linn_mccormack_case_court_strikes_down_idaho_s_abortion_laws.html.

Ura, Alexa. "U.S. Supreme Court Overturns Texas Abortion Restrictions." *The Texas Tribune*, 27 June 2016, www.texastribune.org/2016/06/27/us-supreme-court-rules-texas-abortion-case/.

Quenching the Fire Within: Freedom, Oppression, and the Courage to Overcome in James Baldwin's "Notes of a Native Son" and Hanan Al-Shaykh's "The Women's Swimming Pool"

by Chad Curtiss

One of the most tragic traditions of human history has been the pervasive and persistent need to conquer and subjugate one another. Whether determined unequal because of race or gender or some other reason, voices throughout literature cry out both for freedom and for understanding of their oppression. Hanan Al-Shaykh and James Baldwin are two examples of authors who explore the legacy of oppression in a changing world and a new generation. Al-Shaykh's short story "The Women's Swimming Pool" (1982) details the intricacies of being a woman in a male-dominated society, and what "freedom" as a woman in an Islamic society meant for her. Similarly, "Notes of a Native Son" (1955) by Baldwin provides personal context about the emotional toll of a black man living in the Jim Crow South where he is reminded that, in America, freedom does not necessarily mean equality. Both works portray the inner fire that drives the oppressed to seek freedom at any cost, despite the generational ties that threaten to pull them back into oppression.

A large part of oppression is using humiliation to erode self-worth and force an individual or group of people to comply with the oppressor's wishes. In Al-Shaykh's "fundamentalist Islamic [setting] . . . the situation for women [had] deteriorated" (Keuning 12). Her female characters are "victims of an Islamic patriarchy that treats them as second-class citizens, powerless both politically and economically" (Larson 1). In essence, Al-Shaykh's character in "The Women's Swimming Pool" is "a woman with no rights at all, a nonperson" (Larson 3). She is forced to "wear that dress with long sleeves, that head covering over [her] braids, despite the hot wind and the sparse poplars swaying" (Al-Shaykh 1168). However, she draws the line at wearing the same "thick black stockings" that her grandmother wears, a refusal that suggests that the speaker is going to break from tradition. In fact, the speaker's journey to find the women's swimming pool is symbolic of her journey to find her freedom. She begins the story "growing thirsty and dreaming" (1167), and she repeats this phrase several times in the opening paragraphs. When she goes in search of water under the "hot . . . harsh sun," she is frustrated that she cannot "savor its relative coolness" (1167) because her grandmother interrupts her. The harshness of the sun symbolizes the harsh regime of oppression she lives under, while the water represents cool, refreshing freedom. Her grandmother personifies the traditions of her culture that are standing in the way of getting what she wants.

Similarly in the American South, Baldwin's skin color marked him as unequal in "the land of the free." Baldwin describes how his father, "one of the first generation of free men," claimed to be "proud of his blackness" (Baldwin 738). However, this same badge of honor enslaved him within "fixed bleak boundaries to his life . . . [causing him] much humiliation" (738). Baldwin understands his father's humiliation when he himself is told, "We don't serve Negros here" (741). This experience highlights the fact that Baldwin is "black" and "menaced" like his father (738), pushing Baldwin toward the desire "to crush these white faces, as they were crushing [him]" (742). In both of these scenes, the speakers are feeling choked, squelched by their situations, and these intense scenes are pushing them to do things they would not otherwise consider.

Oppression reinforces a narrative of the supremacy of one group through the humiliation and subjugation of another. This humiliation gives rise to an undercurrent of fear as the oppressed begin to question their safety in a culture bent against their best interests. In Al-Shaykh's Islamic patriarchy setting, "[men] think that women are not individuals . . . always part of the family, not as individuals on their own. This is also because they are responsible for the women in every respect, especially financially. This makes them feel that somehow they own women" (Sunderman 10). This societal value trickles down into individual lives through threats and fears in an effort to protect the family's honor and reputation. Along their journey, the speaker and her grandmother are fearful of being caught. The fear is clear when Grandmother says, "If any man were to see you, you'd be done for, and so would your mother and father and grandfather . . . and I'd be done for more than anyone because it's I who agreed to this and helped you" (Al-Shaykh 1168). Grandmother "was frightened they wouldn't go to heaven" (1168) because her religion taught her that the honor of an entire family rests upon the women of the family and their reputations. This is a prime example of how "religion can bestow social status and communal identity" (Joseph 15) in a negative way. These women are trapped in a male-dominated cultural and religious tradition that governs every aspect of their lives, including "marriage, divorce, child custody, and inheritance" (Joseph 15). Unless they submit to the life decided for them, they are at risk of disgracing their families and potentially losing their very lives.

Baldwin describes his father's suffering with the same pervasive and paralyzing fear, as his father routinely warns his children not to trust white people. He admonished that white people "would do anything to keep a Negro down," and Baldwin and his siblings should "have as little to do with them as possible" (740). As an enlightened Northern man, Baldwin was skeptical of his father's warning, until he discovered the "weight of white people" for himself, a weight that "had been for my ancestors and now would be for me an awful thing to live with" (738). He recognizes that this fear leads to bitterness that "helped to kill [his] father" (738) and could also kill him. In both of these examples of fear, the flame of the need for freedom and self-autonomy continues to rise, and, without something to soothe it, the fire will only grow and become more destructive.

Oppression and alienation lead to bitterness. Baldwin reflects on his father's bitterness and understands it as rooted in the trauma he experienced by being black in America, similar to the way veterans struggle with PTSD after returning from war. His father had "lived and died in an intolerable bitterness of spirit" which was frightening to Baldwin as he realizes this bitterness is inescapable for him too. Baldwin explains how he too has contracted this incurable "chronic disease," this shared "rage in the blood," and states that "one has the choice, merely, of living with it consciously or surrendering to it" (741). In a way, Baldwin has to quit fighting against the bitterness and allow himself to work through it in order to heal.

For Al-Shaykh, the contrast between the "dust and mud and the stench of tobacco" and "the cooler . . . waters . . . [inviting her] to bathe in them" shows the depth of the speaker's "obsession, ever since [she] had seen [the ocean] for the first time inside a colored ball" (1168). Even the confinement of the ocean inside the ball is ironic and points to her own imprisonment within her society. However, it is that small glimpse of the ocean (freedom) that encourages her to take the risk to see the real thing for herself. In many ways, the speaker is taking this journey to avoid growing bitter, and, as the story unfolds, her patience begins to wane as she begins to worry if she will reach her goal or not. In keeping with the fire metaphor, Baldwin and Al-Shaykh handle their bitterness differently. Baldwin surrenders to the bitterness that consumes him; however, Al-Shaykh sets out on a journey to quench the burning desire inside of her before it gets out of control.

Hatred is insidious because it is contagious; a natural response to hate is to return hate back. Baldwin imagines that "one of the reasons people cling to their hate so stubbornly is because they sense, once hate is gone, that they will be forced to deal with pain" (735). He recognizes that this is his own struggle after he experiences the danger of the "hatred [he] carried in [his] own heart" (743). However, hatred is a conscious act that requires a decision. When Baldwin realizes that he is feeding his fear-driven hatred toward the whites he encounters, he turns inward and examines why he feels the way he does.

Similarly, when Al-Shaykh's speaker finally reaches her breaking point and cannot stand to wait any longer, she takes her frustration out on her grandmother "wishing to reproach her, to punish her for having insisted on accompanying [the speaker] instead of Sumayya" (1170). Moreover, "It was as though I was taking vengeance on my grandmother for some wrong she did not know about. My patience vanished" (1170). The speaker is frustrated at the process and hassle this day has been, and, in many ways, her grandmother has dragged her down in more ways than one—by constantly complaining, leaning on things, shaming her—yet the speaker presses on, determined to reach her goal. Furthermore, when she sees her grandmother performing the daily prayers in the middle of the street, the speaker momentarily disowns her grandmother, admitting that she "walked off in another direction and stopped looking at her" and she "would have liked to persuade

[her]self that she had nothing to do with [her], that [she] didn't know her" (1171). This symbolizes the speaker's realization that, in order to find the shame-free freedom she is looking for, she will have to turn her back on all that she has known (e.g. her familial and cultural traditions) and embrace a strange new reality.

At the end of the day, both Baldwin and Al-Shaykh are left with a choice. Baldwin can either run away from his fear or isolate himself like his father, but he realizes that "nothing is ever escaped" (751). He also recognizes that "hatred which could destroy so much, never failed to destroy the man who hated," and the only way he would "keep his heart free of hatred and despair" is to accept "life as it is, and men as they are" (751).

Similarly, the speaker of "The Women's Swimming Pool" has an epiphany when she turns around again. The speaker feels "sorry for her [grandmother], for her knees that knelt on the cruelly hard pavement, for her tattooed hands that lay on the dirt" (Al-Shaykh 1171). In essence, she sees the pain and hardship her grandmother has always endured because she believes it is right, and the speaker's compassion toward her grandmother is what actually quenches the anger that is building within her. When the speaker sees "the passers-by staring at her . . . black dress [that] looked shabby," she realizes "how far removed [they] were from these passers-by, from this street, this city, this sea" (1171). The speaker realizes that she cannot just abandon her grandmother in the middle of the street, and, more importantly, she realizes that her grandmother is not someone to lash out at or the enemy. She is a victim of the oppression herself. So, with a renewed understanding, the speaker "approached her [grandmother], and she again put her weight on [the speaker's] hand" (1171). Symbolically, she cannot abandon her cultural heritage yet, even though it weighs her down and seems inconvenient.

In conclusion, the challenges that Al-Shaykh and Baldwin face are essentially the same. However, despite the legacy of humiliation, fear, bitterness, and hatred that they had been handed, Baldwin offers a beacon of hope by exhorting his generation to rise above skin color and "hold on to the things that [matter]" while looking for "answers only the future would give" (751). Similarly, Al-Shaykh's story ends on a hopeful note, that maybe the speaker has hope of succeeding in her quest now that she is wiser to how her society works and the resources she has at her disposal. In the end, Al-Shaykh and Baldwin depict examples of how generational shifts change and challenge the traditions that do not serve the needs of everyone. The lesson they teach is to lean toward peace in all dealings because anger, hatred, bitterness, and fear are fires that threaten to destroy anyone who possesses them.

Works Cited

Al-Shaykh, Hanan. "The Women's Swimming Pool." 1982. Translated by Denys Johnson-Davies. *The Norton Anthology of World Literature*, edited by Peter Simon, F. Abiola Irele, and Heather James, 2nd shorter ed., vol. 2, Norton, 2009, pp. 1169–71. 2 vols.

Baldwin, James. "Notes of a Native Son." 1955. *The Norton Anthology of World Literature*, edited by Peter Simon, F. Abiola Irele, and Heather James, 2nd shorter ed., vol. 2, Norton, 2009, pp. 737–51. 2 vols.

Joseph, Suad. "Patriarchy and Development in the Arab World," *Gender and Development*, vol. 4, no. 2, 1996, pp. 14–19.

Keuning, Patricia. "Heroic Arabesques: A Profile of Lebanese Novelist Hanan Al-Shaykh," *Bloomsbury Review*, vol. 14, no. 5, 1994, p. 7. Rpt. in *Contemporary Literary Criticism*, edited by Jeffery W. Hunter, vol. 218, Gale, 2006, pp. 11–13.

Larson, Charles. "The Fiction of Hanan al-Shaykh, Reluctant Feminist," *World Literature Today*, vol. 65, no. 1, 1991, pp. 14–17.

Sunderman, Paula. "An Interview with Hanan Al-Shaykh," *Michigan Quarterly Review*, vol. 31, no. 4, 1992, pp. 625-36. Rpt. in *Contemporary Literary Criticism*, edited by Jeffery W. Hunter, vol. 218, Gale, 2006, pp. 6–11.

Contributors

We present the Contributors to the Twenty-Four Edition
of *The Polishing Cloth*
in the order and circumstances of their appearance. . .

PART ONE: SHINY

"Haiti: A Life-Changing Trip" by Mylena Moretti
English 1101
English Composition I
Narration
Timed Essay

"Different From My Mother" by Virginia Edwards
English 1101
English Composition I
Timed Essay

"Melting the Ice Away" by Andrew Ford
English 1102
English Composition II
Timed Essay

"The Light of Happiness" by Leu Nubete
English 1101
English Composition I
Narration/Description

"Coca-Cola's Subliminal Efforts to Unify the World" by Rachael Derby
English 1101
English Composition I
Exposition/Narration

"How Creativity Can Enhance Sustainability: A Review of Daan Roosegaarde's 'A Smog Vacuum Cleaner and Other Magical City Designs'" by Ayesha Siddiqa
English 1101
English Composition I
Review

"The Future of Plastic Recycling: A Review of Mike Biddle's 'We Can Recycle Plastic'" by Ayston Scully
English 1102
English Composition II
Review

"Solar Power" by Benton Reese
English 1102
English Composition II
Argumentative

PART TWO: SHINIER

"Reshaping Elwood's World: How Elwood P. Dowd Reshapes His Life and Maintains Happiness in *Harvey*" by Caitlin Clausen
English 1102
English Composition II
Argumentative

"The Workplace in *Our Miss Brooks*: Discerning Acceptable and Appropriate Behavior at Work" by Andrew Ford
English 1102
English Composition II
Film Analysis

"Some Live to Work, Others Work to Live: Work Values in Guy de Maupassant's 'The Necklace'" by Crystal Kim
English 1102
English Composition II
Literary Analysis

"Female Gothicism and Charlotte Perkins Gilman's 'The Yellow Wallpaper'" by Jada Spencer
Introduction to Women's, Gender, and Sexuality Studies
Literary Analysis

"Positive Flawed Decisions: Decision Making in *The Dick Van Dyke Show*'s 'The Curse of the Petrie People'" by Michelle Martin
English 1102
English Composition II
Analysis Primary Source/ Secondary Source

"A Gladys Kravitz in Every Neighbor: Neighbors in William Faulkner's 'A Rose for Emily' and Angela Robinson's *Professor Marston and the Wonder Women*" by Sofi Taher
English 1102
English Composition II
Analysis Primary Source/ Secondary Source

"Identity in Langston Hughes's *Mulatto* and Alice Walker's 'Everyday Use'" by Hannah Huff
English 1102 Honors
English Composition II
Comparison/Contrast

"A Chilling Resemblance: Emily Grierson in William Faulkner's 'A Rose for Emily' and *Friday the 13th*'s Jason Voorhees" by Jack Hardin
English 1102
English Composition II
Comparison/Contrast

PART THREE: SHINIEST

"The Dakota Access Pipeline: Human Beings Are More Important Than the Economy" by Isabella Coty
English 1101
English Composition I
Research Paper

"A Home For Ninety Days: Addressing Homeless Families in America" by Emily Fritts
English 1101
English Composition I
Research Paper

"The Right To Choose Is the Right Choice" by Audrey Hewett
English 1101 Honors
English Composition I
Research Paper

"Quenching the Fire Within: Freedom, Oppression, and the Courage to Overcome in James Baldwin's 'Notes of a Native Son' and Hanan Al-Shaykh's 'The Women's Swimming Pool'"
By Chad Curtiss
English 2110
World Literature
Literary Analysis

Reginald Abbott, PhD
Rooster Village Farm
October 2018